Do You Want To Get Well?

Books by the Author

Colors of His Grace

Fifty inspirational readings based on the theme- Tapestry

Colors of His Abundance

Devotional readings that provide challenge to daily living in
God's Abundance

In the Morning....Joy

The life story of the author is told through thirty counseling sessions.
The author is both the client and the counselor.

Do You Want To Get Well?

A 31-Day Guide to Daily Devotions

by

Mary Kathryn Clark

Gotham Books

30 N Gould St.
Ste. 20820, Sheridan, WY 82801
https://gothambooksinc.com/

Phone: 1 (307) 464-7800

© 2023 *Mary Kathryn Clark*. All rights reserved.

No part of this book may be reproduced, stored in a retrieval system, or transmitted by any means without the written permission of the author.

Published by Gotham Books (September 13, 2023)

ISBN: 979-8-88775-104-7 (P)
ISBN: 979-8-88775-105-4 (E)

Because of the dynamic nature of the Internet, any web addresses or links contained in this book may have changed since publication and may no longer be valid.

The views expressed in this work are solely those of the author and do not necessarily reflect the views of the publisher, and the publisher hereby disclaims any responsibility for them.

To

Ed, my deceased husband,

who for thirty-two years taught me

the importance of a daily devotional time.

Acknowledgements

To Will and Judy through his encouragement and her computer skills made this book possible

To Brett Adams whose positive support guided me through the steps of publication

To Kevin and Butch for their encouragement to make the financial investment

To Ron and Dot, my loyal friends and prayer warriors

To Marcy, whose weekly visits and sharing food kept me nourished

To Melissa who is my hands and feet in maintaining my home

To Butch and Jenny whose regular visits of sharing dinners and challenging me in Rummikub games

To Andrea, Hildegard and Shirley whose daily phone calls and e-mails made my day brighter

To the Jeff Engler family who graciously helped me through my recent hospitalization and rehabilitation

The Search for Solitude 73

The Limits of Today 77

The Inevitability of Death 81

The Recognition of Abundance..87

The Tediousness of Work 91

The Struggle of Surrender 95

The Doom of Fear 99

The Efficacy of Prayer 103

The Difficulty with Communication 107

The Destruction of Anger...111

The Seriousness of Example 115

The Tenacity of Patience..119

The Toll of Guilt and Resentment...................................123

The Centrality of Purpose 127

The Craving for Relationships 133

The Foolishness of Expectations.....................................137

The Cost of Love...141

Checklist for New Year..145

The Cathedral of Leaves 146

We Are Wonderfully Made...147

Willing to Be Whole 148

About the Author...149

Keys to Wellness

And I will give you the keys of the kingdom of heaven and whatever you bind on earth will be bound in heaven, and whatever you loose on earth will be loosed in heaven.

Matthew 16:19

Our shattered dreams are never random; they are always a piece in a larger puzzle, a chapter in a larger story.

Larry Crabb

Introduction

This book was begun in 2015 and was about 80% completed when I decided I was too old to write another book, so I put it in a box and forgot about it.

A few months ago, I was cleaning out the garage and discovered the box and re-read the manuscript. I felt that God was leading me to complete it.

It was originally typed in Word Perfect, and I was told that it couldn't be converted. I have a friend who had excellent computer skills, and I found the thumb drive which had the entire manuscript on it. She took it home, converted the files and sent them back to me so that I could edit them. It just seemed like a "God-thing".

I am ninety-one years old and a daily quiet time has been a part of my life for many years. I have used all the suggestions made in these thirty-one days.

Especially music has been important to me in my quiet time. The words of the old hymns hold much wisdom and the newer praise songs bring me close to God.

I pray as you journey through these thirty-one days to wellness, that you will experience a new depth of physical, mental and spiritual health.

Mary Kathryn Clark

Do You Want to Get Well?

"Inside the city, near the Sheep Gate, was Bethesda Pool, with five covered platforms or porches surrounding it. Crowds of sick folks— lame, blind, or with paralyzed limbs—lay on the platforms (waiting for a certain movement of the water, for an angel of the Lord came from time to time and disturbed the water, and the first person to step down into it afterwards was healed). One of the men lying there had been sick for thirty-eight years. When Jesus saw him and knew how long he had been ill, he asked him, 'Would you like to get well?'"

"'I can't, sir,' the sick man said, 'for I have no one to help me into the pool at the movement of the water. While I am trying to get there, someone else always gets in ahead of me.' Jesus told him, 'Stand up, roll up your sleeping mat and go on home!' Instantly the man was healed! He rolled up the mat and began walking!"

John 5:2-9 (Living Bible)

The man in this story had been sick for a very long time. He was identified by his sickness; people thought of him as being one who could do nothing for himself. He was dependent on those who passed by to toss a coin in his direction, or say a kind word of sympathy. It is a frightening thing to be well. It means that all of our excuses are gone. It means that, since we are no longer identified with our problem, we are now expected to act on behalf of others and the Lord. If we are healed, our lives would be changed, and we would have to become responsible for making different choices. Do *you* want to get well or would you rather stay sick for just one more day?

Mary Kathryn Clark

Sheila Walsh writes in <u>The Heartache Nobody Sees</u>, "Being healed by Christ teaches you one thing for sure; we are healed to come to others in Jesus' name, offering the same healing. We are no longer at liberty to be part of the problem; we are given the joy of being part of the solution... Those who have been broken and restored by Christ have a God-given ability to connect with others in pain and offer hope and healing. It is one of the greatest privileges of my life to watch the way God uses what was a nightmare to me at the time as a candle in the darkness to others... When Christ heals us, when we get up and walk again, we discover there is work to be done. We have begun to live again!"

"Do you want to get well?" is perhaps the most important question Jesus asked in all of His ministry. I propose that most people will answer "No". We, like the man by the pool, have our long well-rehearsed list of excuses and are so accustomed to our sickness that we don't even consider getting well. Our sickness has become the "norm". We continue living at about 50% and wonder what Jesus was talking about when He spoke of the abundant life filled with joy. We have gotten by so far, why change?

Our list of excuses include: we are too old, too set in our ways, too much trouble, God doesn't care about me personally, and growth and change take too much time and effort. And add to that the belief that we are not supposed to experience excellent physical, social, emotional or spiritual health in this life, that is saved for our spiritual bodies in heaven. So why think about getting well?

Do You Want To Get Well?

The most used excuse is our family of origin. It has been said that 95% of us come from dysfunctional homes and the other 5% is in denial. That levels the playing field. None of us come from perfect homes. We have to give up blaming our parents for our sickness.

I believe we can experience much more health than we currently experience. I believe if we answer Jesus' poignant question with a "Yes", our life will be transformed.

For many years, I had the strong belief that it was possible to get well if I could find the right self-help books, and follow all the suggestions. I had several shelves filled with self-help books, and I faithfully tried many different suggestions, but after the novelty wore off, I was back at square one.

With the help and leadership of the Holy Spirit, He was able to get through to me with the message that I will never find the right self-help program. I had experienced failure because I had thought if I worked hard enough, I could get well.

I finally came to the conclusion that the ONLY thing I could do was to create an environment in which Jesus could perform a miracle in my life and give me health. The man beside the pool was given an instant miracle, and Jesus may do that for you, but in my experience, it is more likely that it is a process in which Jesus works on different areas of my life, and it is a daily "sanctification" through the leadership of the Holy Spirit.

This book is designed as a thirty-one-day program to assist you in preparing an environment in which Jesus can give you health—physically, mentally, emotionally and spiritually. It can be used as a guide to individual growth or in small groups.

Preparing the environment takes discipline and a dogged determination to take the time to be still and listen. When Dallas Cowboys' coach, Tom Landry, was asked how to build a winning team he said, *"My job is to get men to do what they don't want to do, in order to achieve what they've always wanted to achieve."* There must be daily, intentional, definable actions with a clear goal in mind. *"Spend your time and energy in training yourself for spiritual fitness."*

I Timothy 4:7 (Life Application Study Bible)

Training calls for repetitive exercises so that your mind and appropriate muscle groups work together reflexively and automatically, combining endurance and skill. Why train yourself? To become like Christ! Allowing the Holy Spirit to shape you by His disciplines from the inside out, you'll become more like Him. Nobody else can do it for you. You can't inherit it, borrow it, or pay for it. You have to make the most important decision in your life. I want to get well.

We begin by setting aside a daily time of an hour. Preferably it is the same time each day, and if possible, in the same chair. Spiritual power is cumulative. There is a specific plan for each day. It is suggested that you keep a journal and record your responses. Some of the activities are repeated daily.

All of the steps mentioned are ones I have used in my own quiet times over the years. At times one activity has been more meaningful than the other, but all of them have brought me to a time of quiet reflection in my soul and "tilled the ground" for the Holy Spirit to work in my life.

First

Go to the Word of God and pray the prayer from Ephesians that you be given the whole armor of God. When you make the decision to begin these thirty-one devotions, Satan will be extremely nervous and disappointed because he is in eminent danger of losing you. He will use all of his creative suggestions, designed specifically according to your weaknesses, to discourage and deter you.

Read this prayer thoughtfully as you begin your quiet time:

"Finally, be strong in the Lord and in the strength of His might I must put on the whole armor of God, that I may be able to stand against the wiles (schemes) of the devil. For my struggle is not against flesh and blood, but against the rulers, against the powers, against the world forces of darkness, and against the spiritual forces of wickedness in the heavenly places.

Therefore, I will take up the full armor of God, that I may be able to resist in the evil day and having done everything to stand firm.

I will stand firm therefore, having girded my loins with truth and having put on the breastplate of righteousness, and having shod my feet with the preparation of the Gospel of Peace. In addition to all, I will take the shield of faith with which I will be able to extinguish all the flaming missiles of the evil one.

And I will take the helmet of salvation, and the Sword of the Spirit, which is the Word of God with all prayer and petition, I will pray at all times in the Spirit, and with this in view, I will be on the alert with all perseverance and petition for all the saints, And I will pray that utterance may be given to me in the opening of my mouth to make known with boldness the mystery of the Gospel."

In the name of Christ, Amen.

Ephesians 6:10-19 (paraphrased from Revised Standard)

Second

Daily, read this prayer by Liberty Savard, which is a prayer asking God to remove your old nature. If you want to get well, pray that you be willing for God to give you a new nature.

"In the name of Jesus Christ, I bind my body, soul and spirit to the will and purposes of God. I bind myself to the truth of God.

I bind myself to an awareness of the power of blood of Jesus working in my life every day. I bind my mind to the mind of Christ that I can have the thoughts, purposes, and feelings of His heart in me.

I bind my feet to the paths you have ordained for me to walk, God, that my steps will be strong and steady.

I bind myself to the work of the cross with all of its mercy, truth, love, power, forgiveness and dying to self.

In the name of Jesus Christ, I bind the strong man (Satan) and I loose his hold on everything he has ever stolen from me. I rebuke his works and loose the power and effects of every deception, device, and influence he wants to bring against me.

Lord, I repent of wrong attitudes and thoughts, I renounce them now and ask your forgiveness.

I loose every old wrong pattern of thinking, attitude, idea, desire, belief, habit and behavior that may still be working in me. I tear down, crush, smash, and destroy every stronghold I have erected to protect them.

I bind myself to the attitudes and patterns of Jesus Christ. I bind myself to the overcoming behavior and spiritual desires that line up with the fruit of the Holy Spirit.

Father, I loose any stronghold in my life protecting wrong feelings I have against anyone. Forgive me as I forgive those who have caused me pain, loss or grief. I loose any desire for retribution or redress.

In the name of Jesus, I loose the power and the effects of any harsh words (word curses) spoken about me, to me or by me. I loose any strongholds connected with them. I loose all generational bondages and their strongholds from myself. Thank you, Jesus, that you have promised whatsoever I bind and loose on earth will be bound and loosed in heaven. Amen."

Mary Kathryn Clark

Steps one and two are the disciplined steps for building a strong foundation and are repeated daily.

"Therefore, if any man be in Christ, he is a new creature: old things are passed away; behold, all things are become new."

II Corinthians 5:17

Third

Step three brings to mind the issues that may not have been totally surrendered to Christ. These topics represent the most common life experiences. Each of these issues are involved in your new nature and health. An entire book could be written on each topic. Some of the topics may be your issue, and you may need to spend additional time on that topic. Others may not give you a personal challenge. Read each topic thoughtfully, mindfully and prayerfully.

Fourth

The fourth step gives you an opportunity to respond to the challenge. In your journal, you are asked to answer three questions based on the reading. Take your time and think about each question.

Some of you may never have kept a journal and writing may not be easy for you.

You don't have to write long responses… just a few words will suffice. This journal is your private diary, and what you write is not to be read by anyone else. This frees you to be honest. Keep it in a place only known to you.

Fifth

The fifth step is one of inspiration from those who have walked the way and have written words that have assisted them in their walk. Music is therapy for the soul.

How many times have you heard spiritual music played and tears filled your eyes? Music offers relaxation and calmness for the soul. Think about what the words affirm. To listen, Google search the music title and click on YouTube. Be aware of how music brings you closer to God.

David Jeremiah writes, *"'Music is God's therapy for the heart, and the songs of Zion whether old or new- have the ability to encourage us when little else will help.' Are you listening to the right music? Are you saying, 'Singing I go along life's road, praising the Lord, praising the Lord?' 'He put a new song in my mouth, a song of praise to our God!'"*

Psalm 40:3 (RSV)

Sixth

This step enables you to relax into a rhythm of breathing which gives vitality. Put your hands on your stomach, take a deep breath, and feel your stomach extend. Then slowly let the air out and feel your stomach depress. Much has been written about the benefits of deep breathing. It clears the mind, relaxes the body, and lowers blood pressure. Even just a few minutes can have beneficial results. First, practice the act of deep breathing. Then you are given a few words each day to "breathe in and breathe out." Say these words aloud in coordination with your breathing.

"And the Lord God formed man of the dust of the ground, and breathed into his nostrils the breath of life; and man became a living soul."

Genesis 2:7 (King James)

"The spirit of God hath made me, and the breath of the Almighty hath given me life."

Job 33:4 (King James)

Seventh

The final step is to surrender the day to Christ and the leadership of the Holy Spirit in every deed and thought.

"Father, I give this day to you. Direct my feet, use my hands, tune my hearing to the needs of others, use my words to affirm and encourage, and help me to see Your beauty in the world."

Do you want to get well? This book gives you tools to enhance your journey from sickness to wholeness. Use the steps to prepare the environment, and then WATCH to see what Christ does.

He is at His best in the business of transforming lives!

Step One

Read this prayer thoughtfully as you begin your quiet time.

"Finally, be strong in the Lord and in the strength of his might. I must put on the whole armor of God, that I may be able to stand against the wiles (schemes) of the devil. For my struggle is not against flesh and blood, but against the rulers, against the powers, against the world forces of darkness, against the spiritual forces of wickedness in the heavenly places.

Therefore, I will take up the full armor of God, that I may be able to resist in the evil day and having done everything to stand firm.

I will stand firm therefore, having girded my loins with truth and having put on the breastplate of righteousness, and having shod my feet with the preparation of the Gospel of Peace. In addition to all, I will take the shield of faith with which I will be able to extinguish all the flaming missiles of the evil one.

And I will take the helmet of salvation, and the Sword of the Spirit, which is the Word of God with all prayer and petition, I will pray at all times in the Spirit, and with this in view, I will be on the alert with all perseverance and petition for all the saints, And I will pray that utterance may be given to me in the opening of my mouth to make known with boldness the mystery of the Gospel."

Mary Kathryn Clark

In the name of Christ, Amen.

Ephesians 6:10-19 (paraphrased from Revised Standard)

Step Two

Daily, read this prayer by Liberty Savard, which is a prayer asking God to remove your old nature. If you want to get well, pray that you be willing for God to give you a new nature.

"In the name of Jesus Christ, I bind my body, soul and spirit to the will and purposes of God. I bind myself to the truth of God.

I bind myself to an awareness of the power of blood of Jesus working in my life every day. I bind my mind to the mind of Christ that I can have the thoughts, purposes, and feelings of His heart in me.

I bind my feet to the paths you have ordained for me to walk, God, that my steps will be strong and steady.

I bind myself to the work of the cross with all of its mercy, truth, love, power, forgiveness and dying to self.

In the name of Jesus Christ, I bind the strong man (Satan) and I loose his hold on everything he has ever stolen from me. I rebuke his works and loose the power and effects of every deception, device, and influence he wants to bring against me.

Lord, I repent of wrong attitudes and thoughts, I renounce them now and ask your forgiveness.

Mary Kathryn Clark

I loose every old wrong pattern of thinking, attitude, idea, desire, belief, habit and behavior that may still be working in me. I tear down, crush, smash and destroy every stronghold I have erected to protect them.

I bind myself to the attitudes and patterns of Jesus Christ. I bind myself to the overcoming behavior and spiritual desires that line up with the fruit of the Holy Spirit.

Father, I loose any stronghold in my life protecting wrong feelings I have against anyone. Forgive me as I forgive those who have caused me pain, loss or grief. I loose any desire for retribution or redress.

In the name of Jesus, I loose the power and the effects of any harsh words (word curses) spoken about me, to me or by me. I loose any strongholds connected with them. I loose all generational bondages and their strongholds from myself.

Thank you, Jesus, that you have promised whatsoever I bind and loose on earth will be bound and loosed in heaven. Amen."

Steps one and two are the disciplined steps for building a strong foundation and are repeated daily.

"Therefore, if any man be in Christ, he is a new creature: old things are passed away; behold, all things are become new."

II Corinthians 5:17

Step Three

Day One

The Waste of Someday

"And so, dear brothers and sisters, I plead with you to give your bodies to God. Let them be a living and holy sacrifice—the kind He can accept. When you think of what He has done for you, is this too much to ask? Don't copy the behavior and customs of this world, but be a new and different person with a fresh newness in all you do and think. Then you will learn from your own experience how His ways will really satisfy you."

Romans 12:1-2 (Living Bible)

How many times have you said, "*Someday I am going to do that?*" Someday I am going to take a leisurely ride in the country. Someday I am going to organize my recipe box. Someday I am going to invite my neighbors for a cook-out. Someday I am going to put the pictures in the photo album. Someday I am going to take a class in watercolor painting. The list goes on and on. What keeps us from getting the "someday" plans accomplished?

"The real reasons for repeated delays come not from an outside source, but from our own thinking. Procrastination occurs when we want to avoid discomfort or self-doubt," writes Charles Stanley.

Mary Kathryn Clark

So many times, when I have thought of a task that needed to be done like cleaning out the garage, the task in my mind is much bigger than the job itself.

In my mind, I go through the steps to achieve the project, and it seems like a mammoth job. When I actually do the steps, I find it does not take as long as I thought, and it was not nearly as difficult as assumed.

Some people have developed a lifetime habit of procrastination and have thus missed many of the wonderful opportunities God had planned for them. Some have developed the philosophy of *"Don't do anything today that can wait until tomorrow."* Maybe we think if we wait until tomorrow, it will go away or we will have more energy. Neither usually is true.

"Each indecision brings its own delays and days are lost lamenting over lost days. What you can do or think you can do, begin it. For boldness has Magic, Power and Genius in it."

Johann Wolfgang von Goethe (1749-1832)

You may have heard of the Daffodil Principle. One woman with two hands and two feet and one brain began planting daffodil bulbs one at a time over forty years. She did not stop until she had planted 50,000 bulbs over five acres. One day at a time, she had created something of extraordinary magnificence, beauty and inspiration. A mother and daughter observing this beautiful sight said to each other, *"It makes me sad to think of what I could have accomplished if I had a goal, and I had worked on it one day at a time,*" said the mother. The daughter responded, "*Start tomorrow.*"

Stop waiting—until your car or home is paid off, you get a new home or car, your kids leave the house, you finish school, you organize the garage, you clean off your desk, you lose ten pounds, you gain ten pounds, you get married, you get divorced, you retire.

Today is the first day of the rest of your life.

Step Four   Response

1. What have I been putting off?

2. Prioritize that list and begin one today.

3. Am I procrastinating about reading the Bible and my prayer life? Set a new goal.

Step Five   Inspiration: ***Take My life and Let It Be***

> *Take my life and let it be consecrated, Lord, to thee*
> *Take my hands and let them move*
> *At the impulse of thy love, At the impulse of the love.*
> *Take my feet and let them be swift and beautiful for thee;*
> *Take my voice and let me sing*

Mary Kathryn Clark

Always, only, for my King, always only for my King.

Take my silver and my gold, not a mite would I with-hold;

Take my moments and my days, let them flow in ceaseless praise,

Let them flow in ceaseless praise.

Take my will and make it thine, it shall be no longer mine;

Take my heart, it is thine own

It shall be thy royal throne; it shall be thy royal throne.

Words Frances R. Havergal, 1874
Tune Henri A C. Malan

Step Six   Relaxation

Breathe in action; breathe out procrastination

Step Seven   Commitment

Commit the day to Christ and the leadership of the Holy Spirit

Step Three

Day Two

The Willingness to Trust God with Tomorrow

"Therefore, do not be anxious, saying, "What shall we eat?" or "What shall we drink?" or "What shall we wear?" For the Gentiles seek all these things; and your heavenly Father knows that you need them all. But seek first His kingdom and His righteousness, and all these things shall be yours as well. Therefore do not be anxious about tomorrow, for tomorrow will be anxious for itself. Let the day's own trouble be sufficient for the day."

Matthew 6:31-34 (Revised Standard)

Insurance companies thrive on the public's concern about "what if". We spend countless hours thinking about "what if" this happened, what would I do? We live in a world based on a fear mentality. If there is any kind of threat, the public immediately begins to stockpile items, collect items for an emergency or even build a home that is partly underground. I am not saying that we should not exercise reasonable caution, but according to the words from Matthew, we are not to live in fear.

David Wilkerson, in a sermon entitled, "Trusting God With All Your Tomorrows," gives these two contrasting illustrations. How many times

Mary Kathryn Clark

have you asked, *"Why did this happen to me?"*

An elderly woman shared about the day her future changed. She and her husband had enjoyed a wonderful life together when he suffered a stroke. She was her husband's only caregiver and both were homebound because of his condition.

He became depressed and one day he told her how the stroke had robbed him of his hopes and dreams. He said, *"You can't imagine what it is like to just suffer here in bed. All these years I have been robbed of a useful life with no hope for the next day."*

She responded, *"You seem to forget that I was there through it all. You are not the only one who has suffered. I had hopes and dreams too. All my tomorrows were taken away too."* Shortly after that he died, and she continued to be bitter about the "lost years" for the rest of her life.

On the contrary, Paul had been imprisoned and was chained to a Roman guard. This was not exactly a desirable situation. Paul could have said, *"God, after all I have suffered for you and all I have done for you, is this what I get?"* Paul made up his mind to accept things as they were, and he was able to say, *"I can't change my condition. I could very well die in this state. Yet, I know my steps are ordered by the Lord. Therefore I am going to magnify Christ and be a testimony to the world while I am in these chains."* It is believed that Paul brought all of the Roman guards assigned to him to a living relationship with Christ.

What a difference there is in these two illustrations. One was bitter and lived a fruitless life wallowing in life's disappointments, and the other

Do You Want To Get Well?

took the bitterness and turned it into a challenge to serve God through his testimony.

A person who desires to get well can look forward to the tomorrows because he knows, and knows that he knows, that God will keep His word. He knows that all things work together for good and that NOTHING can come through to hurt or harm him until or unless it is God's will for his life.

If we trust God with our tomorrows, worry will not be a part of our life. If you are a worrier, then it is always the worst possible scenario that comes to your mind first. You can soar from distress to disaster in five seconds.

Worry is a thief of your precious time. Most of the things we worry about never happen anyway, or not in the way we imagine. We need to give our worries to God and ask Him to take that burden. We need to be like Scarlett O'Hara and say, *"I'm not going to think about that right now. I'll think about this tomorrow. After all, tomorrow is another day."*

Step Four   Response

1. List some of my "what ifs".

2. What is my biggest fear about tomorrow?

Mary Kathryn Clark

3. Write about something you worried about and then it never happened, or it happened in a very different way than expected.

Step Five   Inspiration: ***I Know Whom I Have Believed***

> *I know not why God's wondrous grace*
> *To me he has made known,*
> *Nor why unworthy, Christ in love*
> *Redeemed me for his own.*
> *I know not how this saving faith*
> *To me he did impart,*
> *Nor how believing in his Word,*
> *Wrought peace within my heart*
> *I know not how the Spirit moves,*
> *Convincing men of sin*
> *Revealing Jesus thro' the Word,*
> *Creating faith in him.*
> *I know not when my Lord may come,*
> *At night or noon-day fair,*
> *Nor if I'll walk the vale with him,*
> *Or meet him in the air.*

Chorus:

> *But I know whom I have believed,*
> *And am persuaded that he is able*
> *To keep that which I've committed*

Do You Want To Get Well?

Unto him against that day.

Based on II Timothy 1:12
Words Daniel W. Whittle, 1883
Tune James McGranahan, 1883

Step Six   Relaxation

Breathe in trust; breathe out worry

Step Seven   Commitment

Commit the day to Christ and the leadership of the Holy Spirit

Step Three

Day Three

The Wisdom of Balance

"And Jesus increased in wisdom (mental), *and in stature* (physical), *and in favor with God (*spiritual) *and man* (social).*"*

Luke 2:52

These few words in Luke are the only words we have to describe the eighteen silent years of Jesus—from the time his parents found their twelve-year-old son in the Temple sitting in the midst of the teachers, listening to them and asking them questions—to his baptism at the age of thirty. Interestingly, these few words penned by Luke describe the perfect balanced life.

Once I heard a presentation that captured my attention. The speaker drew the outline of a horse on the flip chart. The significant thing about the horse was that the four legs were all of different lengths. He labeled the longest leg physical because we give the greatest amount of time taking care of our physical bodies. The next longest was social because most of us are in relationship with people at home and at work. The mental leg was shorter because few of us challenge ourselves daily in this area by reading and problem solving. Most of us allow television to do our reading for us. The shortest leg was labeled spiritual.

How much time do you give daily to the development of your spiritual life through prayer, meditation and Bible study? The speaker pointed out the dysfunction of the horse, and his inability to walk.

In my counseling, before the clients conclude their sessions, they are encouraged to develop a "program" for themselves to keep their lives balanced and to keep themselves in positive fourfold health. The "program" includes their own specific goals for developing their physical, mental, social and spiritual lives. On more than one occasion when a client returned later in need of help, I would ask if they had worked their "program" and always the answer would be negative.

Dr. Leslie Weatherhead includes this prayer in <u>A Private House of Prayer</u>. *"Grant, O Thou Creator and Lover of Perfection, that Thy Holy Spirit may so flow through my mind and body now that all imperfection may disappear and that I may know that perfection of physical, mental, (social), and spiritual health which is Thy will for all Thy creation, I thank Thee, that now, as I pray, thy healing spirit is at work in me. May Thy Spirit's radiance so fill and overflow my being that the lives of others may be cheered and blessed by every contact I make this day. Amen."*

Step Four   Response

1. Draw a four-legged horse and put the appropriate length of the four legs to describe your life.

Do You Want To Get Well?

2. Decide new physical goals such as better eating habits, regular schedule of exercise, proper rest; plan new social goals such as meet a friend for lunch, make a telephone call if you are feeling lonely; plan new mental goals such as take a class, learn a new skill, read a book, play competitive games; decide new spiritual goals such as join a Bible study group, have a daily quiet time, invite someone to be your prayer partner.

3. Ask one person to be your accountability partner. Tell them your goals and your anticipated time to accomplish them.

Step Five   Inspiration: ***Open My Eyes***

Open my eyes that I may see
Glimpses of truth thou hast for me;
Place in my hands the wonderful key
That shall unclasp, and set me free:
Silently now I wait for thee, Ready, my God, thy will to see;
Open my eyes, illumine me, Spirit divine!
Open my ears that I may hear, Voices of truth
thou sendest clear;
And while the wave-notes fall on my ear,
Everything false will disappear:
Silently now I wait for thee, Ready, my God, thy will to see;
Open my ears, illumine Me, Spirit divine!
Open my mouth and let me bear

Mary Kathryn Clark

Gladly the warm truth everywhere;

Open my heart, and let me prepare

Love with thy children thus to share:

Silently now I wait for thee, Ready my God, thy will to see

Open my heart, illumine me, Spirit divine!

Words and tune Clara H. Scott, 1895

Step Six   Relaxation

Breathe in balance, breathe out disharmony

Step Seven   Commitment

Commit the day to Christ and the leadership of the Holy Spirit

Step Three

Day Four

The Gift of Encouragement

"Don't use bad language. Say only what is good and helpful to those you are talking to, and what will give them a blessing."

Ephesians 4:29 (Living Bible)

"Set a guard over my mouth, O Lord, keep watch over the door of my lips!"

Psalm 141:3 (Revised Standard)

"Some people like to make cutting remarks, but the words of the wise soothe and heal."

Proverbs 12:18 (Living Bible)

"*A little word in kindness spoken,*
A motion or a tear,
Has often healed the heart that's broken
And made a friend sincere.
Then deemed it not an idle thing
A pleasant word to speak;

The face you wear- the thoughts you bring-
The heart may heal or break."

From "A Little Word" by Daniel Clement Colesworthy

Jesus affirmed everyone with whom He came in contact with. He never saw the person for who he was, but for who he could become. That is why people followed Him by the masses. They had never had anyone look at them as Jesus did. How different our world and our homes would be if everyone looked at each other on the basis of who they could be rather than who they were. What a positive affirmation!

When I am at a good place, and I know I am affirmed by God, then it is easy for me to affirm others. When my cup is full, I can easily give others a compliment or give an encouraging word.

The reverse is also true. Hurt people hurt other people. When nothing is right with me, it is easy for me to give others a difficult time. When we hurt, we seem to have a desire to want others to hurt.

Have you gotten a phone call early in the morning and someone said an affirming word and you responded, *"That made my day!"* That is the joy of an encourager. Go out and help others have a good day by giving them an affirmation of who they are or what they are doing. Children respond beautifully to praise and affirmation. It is said that if a first-grade teacher praises something that the child wears, the child will want to wear it every day to school.

Do You Want To Get Well?

Florence Littauer in <u>Silver Boxes,</u> raises these questions:

Do you know someone who has
A song waiting to be sung?
Some art waiting to be hung?
A piece waiting to be played?
A scene waiting to be staged?
A tale waiting to be told?
A book waiting to be sold?
A rhyme waiting to be read?
A speech waiting to be said?
If you do, don't let them die with the music still in them.

It just might be your words of affirmation that unlock the treasure.

Step Four   Response

1. Who do I need to affirm today?

2. Think of people in your life who have affirmed you and how did that make you feel?

3. If you said a critical word to someone yesterday or the day before, call them and apologize. Write your response to this call.

Mary Kathryn Clark

Step Five   Inspiration: *We Are One in the Spirit*

We are one in the Spirit; we are one in the Lord

We are one in the Spirit; we are one in the Lord.

And we pray that all unity may one day be restored.

And they'll know we are Christians by our love, by our love,

Yes, they'll know we're Christians by our love.

We will walk with each other; we will walk hand in hand.

We will walk with each other; we will walk hand in hand.

And together we'll spread the news that God is in our land.

And they'll know we are Christians by our love, by our love,

Yes, they'll know we are Christians by our love.

Text and Music by Peter Scholtes
Tune St. Brendan's

"By this everyone will recognize that you are My Disciples, if you love one another."

John 13:35 (Modern Language)

Step Six   Relaxation

Breathe in affirmation, breathe out criticism

Step Seven   Commitment

Commit the day to Christ and the leadership of the Holy Spirit

Step Three

Day Five

The Need for Connection

"I am the vine; you are the branches. Those who remain in me, and I in them, will produce much fruit. For apart from me you can do nothing."

John 15:5

If you have plants or bushes around your house, you know the importance of staying connected to the root and the value of pruning. After pruning you have a pile of branches and leaves which if left for a day or two will shrivel and die. John has no problem dealing with absolutes. He said apart from God, we can do <u>nothing</u>, not a little, not something, not a portion, John says <u>nothing</u>. That is a troubling thought.

We all have our most effective ways of connecting with God. One of the most meaningful ways for me is through nature. In the beauty of nature, I sense the harmonious interaction of all the elements and forces of life, and that gives me a sense of unity with all of life. For me to be close to God, I have to spend time in nature.

"Love all God's creation, both the whole and every grain of sand. Love every leaf, every ray of light. Love the animals, love the plants, love each separate thing. If thou love each thing that wilt perceive the mystery of God in all; and when once thou perceive this, thou wilt

Mary Kathryn Clark

thenceforward grow every day to a fuller understanding of it: until thou come at last to love the whole world with a love that will then be all embracing and universal."

Feodor Dostoevski (1821-1881)

Clarissa Pinkola Estes writes in <u>The Faithful Gardener</u>, *"To be poor and be without trees, is to be the most starved human being in the world. To be poor and to have trees, is to be completely rich in ways that money can never buy."*

Trees have a natural defense system to the winds and the storms. There is more hidden under the ground than is exposed on top of the ground. The root system gives stability, and the flexibility of the trunk keeps it from being broken in the raging storms.

Tree branches are dependent on the trunk for nourishment and life. If I am rooted in God's truth, I can withstand life's storms. In nature God has no favorites. He loves every part of His creation and values each animal and plant. Thankfully, God loves each of His children unconditionally.

Those people who had the good fortune of being born on a farm have a daily appreciation of birth and death; they experience total dependence on the weather for good growing seasons; and they have an appreciation for God who is the provider. They live close to the earth and at night can stand in darkness and look at the brilliant stars in the heaven. A farmer is totally dependent on God for rain, good growing seasons and

Do You Want To Get Well?

moderate temperatures. Would that all of us could have a brief time on a farm and experience that dependence on God.

Step Four   Response

1. Am I connected to God at this moment? If your answer is Yes, list some of the fruits of your ministry.

2. If I am not connected, what do I need to do to "connect"?

3. Describe a meaningful time in nature when you felt close to God.

Step Five   Inspiration: _**This is My Father's World**_

> _This is My Father's world, And to my list'ning ears;_
> _All nature sings, and round me rings, The music of the spheres._
> _This is my Father's world, I rest me in the thought_
> _Of rocks and trees, of skies and seas; His hands the wonders_
> _wrought._
>
> _This is my Father's world, The birds their carols raise;_
> _The morning light, the lily white, Declare their Maker's praise._
> _This is my Father's world, He shines in all that's fair;_
> _In the rustling grass I hear him pass, He speaks to me_
> _everywhere._
>
> _This is my Father's world, O let me ne'er forget_

35

Mary Kathryn Clark

That though the wrong seems oft so strong, God is the ruler yet.

This is my Father's world, The battle is not done;

Jesus who died shall be satisfied, And earth and heaven be one.

Words Maltbie D. Babcock, 1901
Tune Franklin L. Sheppard, 1915

Step Six   Relaxation

Breathe in connection; breathe out brokenness

Step Seven   Commitment

Commit the day to Christ and to the leadership of the Holy Spirit

Step Three

Day Six

The Agony of Pain

"And God shall wipe away all tears from their eyes; and there shall be no more death, neither sorrow, nor crying, neither shall there be any more pain: for the former things are passed away."

Revelation 21:4

"They are absorbed in their own pain and grief."

Job 14:22

I have suffered physical abuse from a father and from a husband. I have endured emotional abuse, but nothing has brought me to my knees more than physical pain. After a knee replacement which did not go well, there was intense pain for about four months and even fifteen years later, there is mild pain and discomfort. During those months immediately after surgery, I was on heavy doses of pain medication. During those days, I could not pray and make a connection with God. I was dependent on friends who daily upheld me in prayer.

My mental alertness was clouded because of the medication, and my emotional state was one of depression and lethargy.

Mary Kathryn Clark

"Sometimes the greatest growth comes through pain, but it's not the pain that helps me grow, it's my response to it. Will I suffer through the experience and continue as before or let the pain inspire changes that help me grow?"

Lessons I learned through the pain were gratitude for less pain, tolerance for those who suffer pain, and the challenge to maintain good physical health through the aging years.

The relationship between pain and growth seems to be a universal truth. The only way we grow is for the pain intensity to reach a point that we choose to make a change.

I had been experiencing pain in my hip and went to the doctor for an acupuncture treatment. He talked to me about the emotions I was experiencing in a special relationship. He suggested that I was stuffing feelings about what I wanted to say and did not have enough courage to say them. We role played the conversation, and he said if I would have this conversation, it would alleviate the pain in my hip.

Toxic emotions can cause pain.

"Rheumatoid arthritis is often associated with holding onto resentments and hostility, especially in connection with authority...Since we all experience anger and hostility from time to time, you needn't fear these emotions- it's not the emotions themselves but an inability to directly express and resolve the anger and resentment that can bring on the illness. It's as if the unexpressed emotional energy becomes 'stuck' in the joints."

Do You Want To Get Well?

There was a season in my life where I suffered migraine headaches. At that same time, I was experiencing stress in my marriage and in my job. My busy involvement did not allow me to address the real issues.

One Sunday I ended my teaching a class of women by saying, "*I wish you pain.*" Some years later I met a woman who had been there that Sunday, and she said I have never forgotten what you said. I made the statement because I believe that we grow only through our pain. When we realize that we are not self-sufficient, we reach out to God. I also believe that if we do not learn our lesson the first time, the event will be repeated until we learn the lesson.

Step Four   Response

1. What has been the most painful time in my life?

2. How did I deal with that pain?

3. What lessons did I learn from the pain?

Step Five   Inspiration: ***I Need Thee Every Hour***

> *I need thee every hour, Most gracious Lord,*
> *No tender voice like thine, Can peace afford.*
> *I need thee every hour, Stay thou nearby;*

39

Mary Kathryn Clark

Temptations lose their pow'r, When thou art nigh.

I need thee every hour in joy or pain

Come quickly and abide, Or life is vain.

I need thee every hour, Teach me thy will;

Thy promises so rich, In me fulfill

I need thee every hour, Most Holy One;

O make me thine indeed, Thou blessed Son.

I need thee, Oh I need thee; Every hour I need thee!

O bless me now, my Savior, I come to thee.

Words Annie S. Hawks, 1872
Tune Robert Lowry, 1872

Step Six   Relaxation

Breathe in health, breathe out pain

Step Seven   Commitment

Commit the day to Christ and to the leadership of the Holy Spirit

Step Three

Day Seven

The Desire to Control

"If any of you wants to be my follower, let him deny himself and take up his cross and follow me."

Matthew 16:24

The first requirement Jesus gives to be His follower is to deny himself. What does that mean? It does not mean we are to deny our personality which is God-given. It means we are to give up being the center of our being and always wanting our way. God says to be my follower, you must give the right to control your life to me and trust me that I will always do what is the very best for you. This is the key to surrendering your life to Christ.

The need to control is probably the most powerful motivator of behavior known to man. It can be traced back to the Garden of Eden. Adam and Eve wanted to control by putting themselves in the center of their lives, or they wanted to be their own gods. When the Sin-disease came into the environment of the Garden, the atmosphere changed, and it has never been the same since.

The battle of "whose I am" began in the Garden and continues in the heart of every human being. Our culture has programmed us to believe that we belong to ourselves. I am the Captain of my ship and what I do only affects me. We have accepted the myth that if we buy one more self-help book, we can figure out life, and we will be able to handle it on our own.

One of the most true and yet difficult paradoxes in life to accept is—To lose control is to gain control. To face losing control feels powerless, helpless, weak, uncertain, scared, dependent, disabled and paralyzing. Who wants to feel this way? And yet, all Scripture teaches that we have to surrender and give up our goals and ideas if we are to do God's will in our life. We have to trust that God knows what He is doing and that He will never ask us to do anything that He does not prepare us to accomplish. If we only do His will, we will never make a mistake. We will never find ourselves out on a side road realizing we had made a mistake, and then we have to painfully come back and get on track again. So much wasted time, energy and money when we always try to have it our way.

To know His plan, I have to be _willing_ to give up mine. I have to study the Scriptures and become familiar with those who followed God. We will see that all were willing to give up their plans and obey God's directions. I believe that God created each of us for a purpose and if we don't discover that purpose, God may have to wait several generations before He creates another person to fulfill that purpose. It is our awesome responsibility to find our purpose and let Him control our life.

Do You Want To Get Well?

Step Four   Response

1. Who or what controls my life? Clue: What do I give my time and money to?

2. What is the area I most want to hold on to?

3. Think of a time in your life when you felt you were in God's will and were fulfilling your purpose and contrast that with a time when you felt you were on a side road because you were determined to have your own way.

Step Five   Inspiration: *I Surrender All*

> *All to Jesus I surrender, All to him I freely give*
> *I will ever love and trust him, In his presence daily live.*
> *All to Jesus I surrender, Make me, Savior wholly thine;*
> *Let me feel thy Holy Spirit, Truly know that thou art mine.*
> *All to Jesus I surrender, Lord, I give myself to thee;*
> *Fill me with thy love and power, Let thy blessing fall on me.*
> *I surrender all, I surrender all*
> *All to thee, my blessed Savior, I surrender all.*

Judson W. Van DeVenter, 1896
Winfield S. Weeden, 1896

Mary Kathryn Clark

Step Six   Relaxation

Breathe in God's will, breathe out My way

Step Seven   Commitment

Commit the day to Christ and to the leadership of the Holy Spirit

Step Three

Day Eight

The Cleansing of Forgiveness

"I will remember their sins no more."

Hebrews 8:12

"O Lord, you are so good, so ready to forgive, so full of unfailing love for all who ask your aid."

Psalm 86:5

"And what a difference between our sin and God's generous gift of forgiveness. For one man, Adam, brought death to many through his sin. But this other man, Jesus Christ, brought forgiveness to many through God's bountiful gift."

Romans 5:15

How many times have your gone over a hurtful scene and said, *"I'll never forget that!"* Why do we keep "nursing" our hurts and wounds from the past? Why do we keep rehearsing those words we want to say to even the score? Forgiveness, because of Christ's grace, is about forgetting, not remembering.

Jesus is very clear about the necessity of forgiveness. *"If you forgive those who sin against you, your heavenly Father will forgive you. But if you refuse to forgive others, your Father will not forgive your sins."*

Matthew 6:14-15

He gives a promise to forgive us, but it is conditional. We must forgive others.

I once heard a minister say, *"You can't get any closer to God than to your bitterest enemy."*

At first, I didn't want to believe that spiritual principle. But I have to realize that if the horizontal line is filled with broken relationships, then I don't have a clear vertical line to God.

My deceased husband in his devotional book, "<u>Swinging on the Front Gate</u>," wrote, *"If I am to be freed from my sins, I must in turn set free all who have sinned against me. It is only when God has forgiven our sins that we find ourselves completely free even as if we had not sinned. To be forgiven by God is to be set free as the air we breathe and as the bird which has been released from its cage. Watch it fly! In the heavens it soars chirping and singing to let the world know that it is free, free, free again."*

Max Lucado says, *"God doesn't just forgive, he forgets... For all the things he does do, this is one thing he refuses to do. He refuses to keep a list of my wrongs."*

Do You Want To Get Well?

Step Four   Response

1. Who do I need to forgive today?

2. List things in myself I need to forgive.

3. Write a prayer of thanksgiving to God that He does not keep a list of my wrongs.

Step Five   Inspiration: ***Down At the Cross***

> *Down at the cross where my Savior died,*
> *Down where for cleansing from sin I cried,*
> *There in my heart was the blood applied, Glory to his name.*
> *I am so wondrously saved from sin, Jesus so sweetly abides within,*
> *There at the cross where he took me in; Glory to his name.*
> *Oh, precious fountain that saves from sin,*
> *I am so glad I have entered in;*
> *There Jesus saves me and keeps me clean; Glory to his name.*
> *Come to the fountain so rich and sweet,*
> *Cast thy poor soul at the Savior's feet*
> *Plunge in today and be made complete; Glory to his name.*
> *Glory to his name, Glory to his name;*

Mary Kathryn Clark

There to my heart was the blood applied; Glory to his name.

Elisha A. Huffman, 1878
John H. Stockton, 1878

Step Six   Relaxation

Breathe in forgiveness, breathe out remembering

Step Seven   Commitment

Commit the day to Christ and to the leadership of the Holy Spirit

Step Three

Day Nine

The Equality of Time

"Everything that happens in this world happens at the time God chooses. He sets the time for birth and the time for death, the time for planting and the time for pulling up, the time for killing and the time for healing, the time for tearing down and the time for building. He sets the time for sorrow and the time for joy, the time for mourning and the time for dancing, the time for making love and the time for not making love, the time for kissing and the time for not kissing. He sets the time for finding and the time for losing, the time for saving and the time for throwing away, the time for tearing and the time for mending, the time for silence and the time to talk. He sets the time for love and the time for hate, the time for war and the time for peace."

Ecclesiastes 3:1-8

In God's eyes, time is not a problem.

Frederick Buechner gives these ideas about time in Listening to Your Life. *"It is by its content rather than its duration that a child knows time, by its quality rather than its quantity- happy and sad times, the time the rabbit bit your finger... the time you were crying yourself to sleep when somebody came and lay down beside you in the dark for comfort.*

Mary Kathryn Clark

Childhood's time is Adam and Eve's time before they left the garden for good and from that time on divided everything into before and after. It is the time before God told them that the day would come when they would surely die with the result that from that point on they made clocks and calendars for counting their time out like money and never again lived through a day of their lives without being haunted somewhere in the depths of them by the knowledge that each day brought them closer to the end of their lives."

How different it is for us. Most of the time we feel that Time is our Master and controls us. We either have too much time and are bored and depressed, or we don't have enough time to get the necessary tasks completed.

If we do not want to do something, we say, *"I don't have time for that."* If we are busy, but we want to do something, we say,

"I'll make time for that."

If we are competing in a game or sport, we do not want to hear,

"Time's up."

When we are doing something, we enjoy, *"Time flies."*

When we are in love, *"Time stands still."*

As we get older, we hasten the aging process by feeling that

"Time is running out."

We are with a true friend, and we do not want to hear,

"It's time to leave."

Do You Want To Get Well?

None of these statements have anything to do with time on the clock. Time is a state of mind, and I have control of that.

There is an equality of time. We all have the same amount of time every day. What we do with it is our choice. What we think about Time is our decision.

Help me to remember that I have all the time I need.

Step Four   Response

1. Do I feel that Time controls me or that I have control over Time?

2. Look at the last twenty-four hours. Did I use my time wisely? Being objective, how could I have used the time more wisely? Make three columns titled,—for God, for others, for myself, as a way to observe your use of time.

3. Develop new goals for time management.

Step Five   Inspiration: ***Moment By Moment***

> *Dying with Jesus, by death reckoned mine;*
> *Living with Jesus, a new life divine;*
> *Looking to Jesus till glory doth shine,*
> *Moment by moment, O Lord, I am thine.*

51

Mary Kathryn Clark

Never a trial that he is not there,
Never a burden that he doth not bear;
Never a sorrow that he doth not share,
Moment by moment I am under his care.
Never a weakness that he doth not feel,
Never a sickness that he cannot heal;
Moment by moment in woe or in weal,
Jesus my Savior abides with me still.
Moment by moment I'm kept in his love,
Moment by moment I've life from above;
Looking to Jesus till glory doth shine;
Moment by moment, O Lord, I am thine.

Daniel W. Whittle, 1893
May Whittle Moody, 1893

Step Six   Relaxation

Breathe in time enough, breathe out rushing

Step Seven   Commitment

Commit the day to God and to the leadership of the Holy Spirit

Step Three

Day Ten

The Folly of Assumptions

Webster states that assumptions are the "suppositions that something is true." We give energy to support our suppositions. We allow them to dictate our behaviors and ruin our relationships. We base our perception of reality on the fact that they are truth not fiction. We have been known to argue for their validity and their truth. Many of them are the same things we heard our parents say. Not one of them can be substantiated.

My best is still not good enough.
I have been hurt too deeply to ever heal.
If I work hard enough and long enough, life will turn out right.
Others have more talent and skills than I do.
I have to do more than my share of "taking care" in order to be loved.
There will not be enough money to last through my lifetime.
You have to get all the jobs finished to perfection before you can play.
God is disappointed if I do not get it right.
I will ultimately find the way to be happy all the time.
I am only lovable when I meet someone else's expectations.
These faulty assumptions have robbed me of a peace and freedom for which I have searched all my life.

Mary Kathryn Clark

Isn't it amazing that we can go through life and not have these perceptions checked out with truth?

Growth is a process and life is all about learning lessons. I am grateful that one is never too old to trade old faulty perceptions for those that match up with truth.

Step Four   Response

1. Which of the list above are your assumptions? Add additional ones that are yours.

2. Take one faulty assumption a day and ask God to take it out of your thinking and replace it with truth.

3. Read Psalm 139 to find the truth about who you are and how much God loves you.

Step Five   Inspiration: ***Be Thou My Vision***

> *Be thou my vision, O Lord of my heart;*
> *Naught be all else to me, save that thou art;*
> *Thou my best thought, by day or by night,*
> *Waking or sleeping, thy presence my light*
> *Be thou my wisdom, and thou my true word;*

I ever with thee and thou with me Lord;

Thou my great Father, I thy true son,

Thou in me dwelling.

And I with thee one

Riches I heed not, or man's empty praise,

Thou mine inheritance, now and always;

Thou and thou only, first in my heart, High King of heaven

my treasure thou art.

High King of heaven, my victory won,

May I reach heaven's joys, O bright heav'n's Son!

Heart of my own heart, whatever befall,

Still be my vision, O Ruler of all.

Mary Byrne, 1905
Traditional Irish Melody

Step Six   Relaxation

Breathe in truth, breathe out assumptions

Step Seven   Commitment

Commit your day to God and to the leadership of the Holy Spirit

Step Three

Day Eleven

The Power of Words

"He who guards his mouth, preserves his life, but he who opens wide his lips shall have destruction."

Proverbs 13:3

"Death and life are in the power of the tongue: and they that love it shall eat the fruit thereof."

Proverbs 18:20-21

Jesus said, *"Those things which proceed out of the mouth come from the heart, and they defile a man. For out of the heart proceed evil thoughts, murders, adulteries, fornications, thefts, false witness, blasphemies. These are the things which defile a man."*

Matthew 15:18-20

"The tongue of the wise promotes health."

Proverbs 12:18

Mary Kathryn Clark

Liberty Savard in <u>Shattering Our Strongholds</u> says our words are either a blessing or a curse. Think about that. Every time you open your mouth, you are either blessing or cursing the person you are talking with.

We remember words for years. Can you think of a person who said something that hurt your feelings or embarrassed you? You can go back to the spot where you were when they said those words, and you can remember how you felt. On the contrary, you can remember someone who called and affirmed you and your response was, *"You've made my day."*

In <u>Listening to Your Life</u>, Frederick Buechner penned these words, *"Words written fifty years ago, a hundred years ago, a thousand years ago, can have as much of this power today as ever they had to come alive for us and in us and to make us more alive within ourselves. That, I suppose, is the final mystery as well as the final power of words: that not even across great distances of time and space do they ever lose their capacity for becoming incarnate. And when these words tell of virtue and nobility, when they move us closer to that truth and gentleness of spirit by which we become fully human, the reading of them is sacramental; and a library is as holy a place as any temple is holy because through the words which are treasured in it the Word itself becomes flesh again and again and dwells among us and within us, full of grace and truth."*

For me, the time I am most likely to talk too much is when I am anxious in my soul and when I am uncomfortable with the people I am with. Talking seems to be a way to relieve anxiety.

Do You Want To Get Well?

When I am serene in my spirit, I can be a good listener with no need to talk. Or when I do speak, my words have meaning and significance.

Proverbs even says that there is a relationship between my words and my health. A hypochondriac is constantly talking about their illnesses, and no one likes to be around them. Everyone likes to be around someone who is positive and uplifting and can inject a bit of humor into this sin-filled world.

Step Four   Response

1. Think about words which "cursed you" and who said them and when they were said. Write them down and ask God to remove the memory.

2. Think about someone who affirmed you and by their faith and trust in you, allowed you to believe in yourself. Write their words down.

3. Think about the words you spoke yesterday. Did any of them harm or affirm anyone? What was their response? Is an apology needed?

Step Five   Inspiration: *Living for Jesus*

> *Living for Jesus a life that is true,*
> *Striving to please him in all that I do,*
> *Yielding allegiance, glad hearted and free,*

Mary Kathryn Clark

This is the pathway of blessing for me.

Living for Jesus who died in my place,

Bearing on Calv'ry my sin and disgrace,

Such love constrains me to answer his call,

Follow his leading and answer his call.

Living for Jesus thro' earth's little while,

My dearest treasure the light of his smile,

Seeking the lost ones he died to redeem,

Bringing the weary to find rest in him.

O Jesus, Lord and Savior, I give myself to thee;

For thou, in thine atonement,

Didst give thyself for me; I own no other Master,

My heart shall be thy throne;

My life I live, henceforth to live, O Christ, for thee alone.

Thomas O. Chisholm, 1917
C. Harold Lowden, 1915

Step Six   Relaxation

Breathe in serenity, breathe out anxiety

Step Seven   Commitment

Commit your day to Christ and to the leadership of the Holy Spirit

Step Three

Day Twelve

The Security of Traditions

"Teach them to your children. Talk about them when you are at home and when you are away on a journey, when you are lying down and when you are getting up again. Write them on the doorposts of your house and on your gates, so that as long as the sky remains above the earth, you and your children may flourish in the land the Lord swore to give your ancestors."

Deuteronomy 11:19-21

Traditions can be a paradox. They give a family security and individuality because traditions distinguish them from other families. They may be the only family that does it a certain way and that makes family memories special. Traditions can cause us not to be willing to change, thus growth is inhibited.

A long time ago, I heard a story about a young bride who was preparing to cook a ham for the holidays. She remembered that her mother always cut off the hock before putting it in the roasting pan. The young woman questioned the procedure and called her mother to ask why she did this. The mother said, *"My mother always did it that way."* The mother being curious called her mother and asked why she had done this and she

Mary Kathryn Clark

replied, *"My pan was small, and I had to cut off the hock end to get it in the pan."* The validity of some traditions may need to be questioned.

In my marriage counseling, traditions are discussed. Often the first Christmas together brings up family traditions. The man offers to go get the pine Christmas tree. The woman says, *"But we always had spruce."*

Perhaps compromise is in order. Pine one year and spruce the next.

A year or so ago, I had a pair of shoes with laces that would not stay tied. I knew how to tie my shoes. I had done it one way for sixty-four years. A friend taught me how to double loop before you tie and then double tie. A little thing, but a tradition was changed.

We tend to hold on to religious ideas we have had since childhood. Our earthly father is our first concept of God. For me, God was someone who expected me to work hard, get it right, and if you did not, there were consequences to pay. That was just what my earthly father had taught me. It took effort, counseling, determination and willingness to change that concept. The God of the New Testament is portrayed in Christ as a loving Father, full of compassion, and one who wants more good for me as His child than I can imagine.

Deuteronomy gives us suggestions as to how to establish traditions in the home. We are to teach spiritual teachings both day and night. Every child has a right to hear his mother and father pray aloud. Families that attend church are likely to be more stable. Young people who have their social friends at church are less likely to be users of drugs and alcohol.

Do You Want To Get Well?

Questions about faith, behaviors, and God should originate and be answered at home.

The sum total of our being today is affected by the traditions in our life.

"And profited in the Jews' religion above many my equals in mine own nation being more exceedingly zealous of the tradition of my fathers."

Galatians 1:14

Step Four   Response

1. Make two columns... one for the traditions you have continued in your family and one for the traditions you have dropped.

2. List the traditions you have created for you and your family today.

3. Be specific about the ways your family incorporates the teaching from Deuteronomy.

Step Five   Inspiration: ***O God Our Help in Ages Past***

O God, our help in ages past, Our hope for years to come,
Our shelter from the stormy blast, And our eternal home.
Under the shadow of thy throne, Thy saints have dwelt secure:
Sufficient is thine arm alone, and our defense is sure.

Mary Kathryn Clark

Before the hills in order stood, Or earth received her frame,

From everlasting thou are God, To endless years the same.

A thousand ages in thy sight, Are like an evening gone:

Short as the watch that ends the night, Before the rising sun.

Time, like an ever rolling stream, Bears all its sons away;

They fly, forgotten, as a dream, Died at the op'ning day.

O God our help in ages past, Our hope for years to come,

Be thou our guard while life shall last, And our eternal home.

Isaac Watts, 1719
William Croft, 1708

Step Six   Relaxation

Breathe in beliefs, breathe out unbeliefs

Step Seven   Commitment

Commit your day to Christ and to the leadership of the Holy Spirit

Step Three

Day Thirteen

The Wonder of Attitude

"Casting down imaginations, and every high thing that exalteth itself against the knowledge of God, and bringing into captivity every thought to the obedience of Christ."

II Corinthians 10:5

Paul suggests in this verse that it takes warfare, hard work, concentration and discipline to bring our attitudes under control. One moment I can be discouraged and see nothing positive and in the next hour, if a circumstance changes, my attitude is different.

A friend told me of an incident when she was upset. She made a list of all the things she was unhappy about and put the paper in the dresser drawer. On another day, when she was feeling good, she made a gratitude list. When she compared the two lists, they were identical.

The AA program has a descriptive saying about negative thinking. They call it "stinking thinking". Negative thoughts cause depression and disease in the body, mind, and soul.

"Be careful what you think, because your thoughts control your life."

Proverbs 4:23

Mary Kathryn Clark

It is not what is going on, it is what I think about it.

When I am upset, it is because of what I am thinking.

Life is 10% what happens to me and 90% how I react to it. As you look at your behavior, do you mostly act or react?

"Finally, brethren, whatsoever things are true, whatsoever things are honest, whatsoever things are just, whatsoever things are pure, whatsoever things are lovely, whatsoever things are of good report; if there be any virtue, and if there be any praise, think on these things."

Philippians 4:5

"As a man thinketh in his heart; so is he."

Proverbs 23:7

"But think on me when it shall be well with thee, and show kindness, I pray, unto me."

Genesis 40:14a

Step Four   Response

1. What negative subject do I obsess about?

2. What helps me stop negative thinking?

Do You Want To Get Well?

3. What conditions are necessary for me to stay in positive thinking?

Step Five Inspiration: ***I Have Decided to Follow Jesus***

I have decided to follow Jesus,
I have decided to follow Jesus,
I have decided to follow Jesus,
No turning back, No turning back.
Tho none go with me, I still will follow,
Tho none go with me, I still will follow,
Tho none go with me, I still will follow,
No turning back, no turning back.
My cross I'll carry till I see Jesus,
My cross I'll carry till I see Jesus,
My cross I'll carry till I see Jesus,
No turning back, I'll follow him.

Garo Christians
John Clark
William J. Reynolds, 1959

Step Six Relaxation

Breathe in positive thoughts, breathe out negative thoughts

Step Seven Commitment

Commit the day to Christ and to the leadership of the Holy Spirit

Step Three

Day Fourteen

The Ecstasy of Freedom

"So if the Son sets you free, you shall be free indeed."

John 8:36

One of my favorite places to frequent is the small mountain stream near the hemlock forest. Usually, I lean against the small railing of the foot bridge and listen to the crystal-clear water gurgling over the smooth rocks. But this day, I decided to sit on the bridge. My feet dangled as a small child's feet. There was not a sound except the music of the water and the clear notes of music from a bird in the distance. I was far away from the din of the city and the tense bodies running back and forth frantically trying to accomplish the responsibilities of the day. I was at peace. I was grateful for the moment when I could just BE, and I did not have to perform or act or behave or control. I was in the freedom of being a worthy child of God whom He created and for whom He had a specific purpose.

As I continued to sit there, I began humming hymns. I had made no effort to memorize the words of the great hymns but was reminded of the story a minister told after returning from Russia. He said in the Christian Russian church people stood wall to wall and sang all of the

Mary Kathryn Clark

verses of the hymn without any hymnals. I didn't get all the words correct and probably had the first verse mixed with the third verse, but it made no difference because I was in the moment, and God was there.

As I walked home, I noticed a large butterfly in a tree close by. It was like a message from God. As a child, I had a recurring dream of being a butterfly in a Mason quart jar. Holes had been punched in the lid so I could breathe. Being in the jar described perfectly the restrictions and pressure I experienced growing up. Now God was showing me that as His child, I was free. The freedom I had longed for all my life is NOW. All I have to do is to become aware of it and acknowledge that freedom is a gift for all those who surrender to Christ.

> *"Stone walls do not a prison make,*
> *Nor iron bars a cage;*
> *Minds innocent and quiet take*
> *That for a hermitage;*
> *If I have freedom in my love,*
> *And in my soul am free,*
> *Angels alone that soar above*
> *Enjoy such liberty."*

Richard Lovelace (1618-1658)

God did not intend for His children to be burdened with responsibility and cares which create tense bodies and confused thinking.

Do You Want To Get Well?

"Stand fast therefore in the liberty wherewith Christ hath made us free, and not be entangled again with the yoke of bondage."

Galatians 5:1

Step Four   Response

1. Make a list of those things which are burdening you now.

2. Describe the last time you felt "free".

3. Memorize **John 8:36** *"Therefore, if the Son makes you free, you shall be free indeed."*

Step Five   Inspiration: *Amazing Love*

> *I'm forgiven because you were forsaken and I'm accepted*
> *You were condemned, I'm alive and well*
> *Your spirit is within me because you died and rose again.*
> *I'm forgiven because you were forsaken and I'm accepted*
> *You were condemned, I'm alive and well*
> *Your spirit is within me, Because you died and rose again.*
> *Amazing love, how can it be that you King would die for me?*
> *Amazing love I know it's true*

Mary Kathryn Clark

That's my joy to honor you in all I do- I honor you.

You are my King, You are my King.

Jesus, you are my King, Jesus, you are my King,

You are my King, Jesus, you are my King.

Chris Tomblin

Step Six   Relaxation

Breathe in freedom, breathe out bondage

Step Seven   Commitment

Commit the day to Christ and to the leadership of the Holy Spirit

Step Three

Day Fifteen

The Search for Solitude

"The next morning Jesus awoke long before daybreak and went out alone into the wilderness to pray."

Mark 1:35

In her book, Intimacy and Solitude, Stephanie Dowrick writes, *"the capacity to be comfortable alone flows from satisfying experiences of being with someone else. What's more important, satisfying experiences of being with someone else fuel a continuing capacity to be alone, without feeling adrift or lonely."*

She describes a balance that is necessary if we are to have spiritual power in our everyday experiences. If Jesus needed time for solitude in order to maintain the balance, how much more do we need it?

It is an interesting concept that being with people drives us to solitude and having our cup filled with solitude drives us to people.

We all have a craving for solitude, yet we seldom label it truthfully. We think we crave relationships, food, fun, money, a different job or a different spouse. There is within each of us a longing for serenity and the knowledge that we are where we are supposed to be, doing what we were created to do. That longing is there because God is within each of us and that longing comes from Him, and until we recognize that, no other craving will satisfy.

Solitude is different from having a quiet time and reading several devotional books. Solitude provides time for me to be alone with God and a time for me to be silent and listen. It is time for me to keep my focus on God's love for me and His purpose for me. It is time for me to take deep breaths and just quiet my mind and soul so that I may be receptive to His word for me.

Do I hear an audible voice? Unlikely, though possible. It is more a feeling of serenity, peace and tranquility. Solitude provides an environment for the Holy Spirit to speak to me or to give me ideas or suggestions of things I can do or a way I should behave. The Holy Spirit may give me a thought that I would never have thought of, thus I know it is divine guidance.

Why don't I make solitude a priority in my life? It takes discipline and a desire to listen to God. It takes patience with an active mind that wants to go all over the place. It takes a belief that it is only through listening that I can know what God's plan is for me.

If you have ever tried making solitude a serious practice in your life, you have experienced the benefits. For me, the amazing thing is that I have tried it, have experienced the benefits and then still give it up for a season because I get too busy or something else becomes a priority.

Do You Want To Get Well?

If you have never tried it, I encourage you to experiment with solitude. Set a time when you will not be disturbed (take the phone off the hook or turn off the cell phone). Begin with reading a few verses of Scripture and then be quiet and allow God to speak to you.

If you have tried it, and this is a time in your life when you are not practicing the discipline, I encourage you to return to the practice.

Each of us needs quality time of solitude, and we also need each other in relationship.

One of life's lessons is to find the appropriate balance between the two.

Step Four   Response

1. Describe a time when you experienced solitude and you knew you were in the presence of God.

2. What is keeping me from having regular times of solitude now?

3. Assess your balance of time between solitude and being in relationship.

Mary Kathryn Clark

Step Five   Inspiration: *As the Deer*

As the deer panteth for the water so my soul longeth after Thee

You alone are my heart's desire, and I long to worship Thee

You alone are my strength, my shield

To You alone may my spirit yield

You alone are my heart's desire, and I long to worship Thee

You're my friend and You are my brother, even though you are

a King

I love you more than any other, so much more than anything

You alone are my strength, my shield

To you alone may my spirit yield

You alone are my heart's desire, and I long to worship Thee

I want you more than gold or silver, Only You can satisfy

You alone are the real joy-giver and the apple of my eye

You alone are my strength and shield,

To You alone may my spirit yield

You alone are my heart's desire, and I long to worship Thee

Martin Nystrom, 1984
Based on Psalm 42

Step six   Relaxation

Breathe in peacefulness, breathe out frenzy

Step seven   Commitment

Commit your day to Christ and to the leadership of the Holy Spirit

Step Three

Day Sixteen

The Limits of Today

In the Sermon on the Mount, Jesus said, *"Do not worry about things. Your Father in Heaven knows all your needs. So do not worry about tomorrow; it will have enough worries of its own. There is no need to add to the troubles each day brings."*

Matthew 6:32-34 paraphrased

"I cannot know what the future will bring. My best hope is every bit as likely to occur as my worst fear, so I have no reason to give more weight to my negative assumptions. All I can do is to make the most of this day."

Thoughts by Frederick Buechner include, *"It is a moment of light surrounded on all sides by darkness and oblivion. In the entire history of the universe, let alone in your own history, there has never been another just like it and there will never be another just like it again. It is the point to which all your yesterdays have been leading since the hour of your birth. It is the point from which all your tomorrows will proceed until the hour of your death.... The point is to see it for what it is because it will be gone before you know it. If you waste it, it is your life that you're wasting, If you look the other way, it may be the moment you've been waiting for always that you're missing. All other days have either disappeared into darkness and oblivion or not yet emerged from the Today is the only day there is."*

"This is the day the Lord has made. We will rejoice and be glad in it."

Psalm 118:23

My thinking can become distorted if I filter past experiences into today. Much energy is lost if I concentrate on tomorrow. These are some questions that have robbed me of the joy of today: Who will be there for me? Who will care? What if I don't have good health? What will it be like if I can't be independent? Will there be enough money? Where should I live?

A meaningful story is related by Brennan Manning. *"A man is being chased by a tiger. He came to the edge of the cliff and there was a rope. He grabbed the rope and swung out over the cliff. He looked up and saw the tiger ready to leap. He looked down and five hundred feet below were sharp jagged rocks. He looked up again and saw two large rats gnawing on the rope that was holding him. He looked straight ahead and there growing out of the cliff was a beautiful, large, ripe strawberry. He plucked the strawberry and ate it. Yum! Yum!"*

If you look to the past, you will be eaten by the tiger. If you look to the future, you will be dashed on the sharp rocks. If you spend energy thinking about your circumstances (the rats), you will waste much time and be exhausted. The ONLY thing you can do is to stay in the moment and enjoy the strawberry.

Do You Want To Get Well?

"How rare it is to be satisfied... not to want something more or something less... not to wish it had been that way or the other... only to accept whatever it is and be satisfied."

Step Four   Response

1. What are you bringing into today from yesterday?

2. What are you worrying about for tomorrow?

3. Draw a picture of a strawberry and color it red. Keep that picture before you as you go through this day.

Step Five   Inspiration: ***This is the Day the Lord Has Made***

This is the day, this is the day that the Lord has made, that the Lord has made.
We will rejoice, we will rejoice and be glad in it and be glad in it,
This is the day that the Lord has made; we will rejoice and be glad in it
This is the day, this is the day that the Lord has made,
Open to us, open to us the gates of God, the gates of God;
We will go in, we will go in and praise the Lord and praise the Lord.
Open to us the gates of God; we will go in and praise the Lord.
Open to us, open to us the gates of God.

Mary Kathryn Clark

You are our God, you are our God; we will praise your name,
we will praise your name;
We will give thanks, we will give thanks for your faithfulness, for your
faithfulness You are our God; we will praise Your name;
We will give thanks for your faithfulness, You are our God,
You are our God; we will praise your name.

Les Garrett
Psalm 118:24

Step Six   Relaxation

Breathe in today, breathe out yesterday

Step Seven   Commitment

Commit the day to Christ and to the leadership of the Holy Spirit

Step Three

Day Seventeen

The Inevitability of Death

"But let me tell you a wonderful secret God has revealed to us. Not all of us will die, but we will all be transformed. It will happen in a moment, in the blinking of an eye, when the last trumpet is blown. For when the trumpet sounds, the Christians who have died will be raised with transformed bodies. And then we who are living will be transformed so that we will never die.

For our perishable earthly bodies must be transformed into heavenly bodies that will never die. When this happens- when our perishable earthly bodies have been transformed into heavenly bodies that will never die- then at last the Scriptures will come true: "Death is swallowed up in victory. O death, where is your victory? O death, where is your sting?"

I Corinthians 15:51-55

Death is a mystery, but the words above come as close as we can get to describing what happens at death. We have an awesome assurance that as a child of God, we have nothing to fear.

In the book, <u>Mister God, This is Anna</u>, we find these words, *"Being dead was nothing to get fussed about. Dying could be a bit of a problem, but*

Mary Kathryn Clark

not if you had really lived. Dying needed a certain amount of preparation and the only preparation for dying was real living, the kind of preparation old Granny Harding had made during her lifetime. We had sat, Anna and I, holding Granny Harding's hand when she died. Granny Harding was glad to die; not because life had been too hard for her, but because she had been glad to live. She was glad that the rest was near; not because she had been overworked, but because she wanted to order, wanted to arrange, ninety-three years of beautiful living; she wanted to play it all over again. 'It's like turning inside out, me dears', she had said... She died happily because she had lived happily."

My husband was a minister for forty-seven years and conducted many funerals. He said the people who mourned the loudest were those who had unfinished business with the deceased.

If we lived every day as if it were our last, we would mend the fences with our neighbors, call a family member and say *"I'm sorry,"* give each child a hug and say, *"I'm so glad God gave you to me."* That is the way you prepare for your death which may be today or tomorrow or fifty years from now.

In my funeral plans, I have requested that this be read:

"I am standing upon the seashore. A ship at my side spreads her white sails to the morning breeze and starts for the blue ocean. She is an object of beauty and strength, and I stand and watch her until at length she hangs like a speck of white cloud just where the sea and sky come

down to mingle with each other. Then someone at my side says: 'There! She's gone!'

Gone where? Gone from sight- that is all. She is just as large in mast and hull and spar as she was when she left my side, and just as able to bear her load of living freight to the place of destination.

Her diminished size is in me, not in her; and just at the moment when someone at my side says, 'There! She's gone!' there are other eyes watching her coming, and other voices ready to take up the glad shout, 'There she comes!' And that is dying."

Author Unknown

Step Four   Response

1. What is my attitude toward my death? Am I fearful?

2. What can I do today to assure my confidence in death?

3. What am I doing today to take care of my physical body which is God's temple but my responsibility to keep in good shape?

Mary Kathryn Clark

Step Five   Inspiration: ***I Was There to Hear Your Borning Cry***

I was there to hear your borning cry,

I'll be there when you are old.

I rejoiced the day you were baptized to see your life unfold.

I was there when you were but a child, with a faith to suit you

well.

In a blaze of light you wandered off to find where demons dwell.

When you heard the wonder of the Word

I was there to cheer you on;

You were raised to praise the living Lord, to whom you now

belong,

If you find someone to share your time and you join your hearts

as one,

I'll be there to make your verses rhyme from dusk 'till the rising

sun.

In the middle ages of your life, not too old, no longer young,

I'll be there to guide you through the night, complete what

I've begun.

When the evening gently closes in and you shut

your weary eyes.

I'll be there as I have always been with just one more surprise.

I was there to hear your borning cry,

I'll be there when you are old.

I rejoiced the day you were baptized, to see your life unfold.

Steve Negley

Do You Want To Get Well?

Step Six   Relaxation

Breathe in life, breathe out fear

Step Seven   Commitment

Commit the day to Christ and to the leadership of the Holy Spirit

Step Three

Day Eighteen

The Recognition of Abundance

God gives abundant mercy. *"The Lord is slow to anger, and rich in unfailing love, forgiving every kind of sin and rebellion."*

Numbers 14:18

God gives abundant provision. *"So the people ate manna for forty years until they arrived in the land of Canaan, where there were crops to eat."*

Exodus 16:35

God gives abundant kindness. *"They refused to listen and did not remember the miracles you had done for them. Instead they rebelled and appointed a leader to take them back to their slavery in Egypt! But you are a God of forgiveness, gracious and merciful, slow to become angry, and full of unfailing love and mercy. You did not abandon them."*

Nehemiah 9:17

God gives abundant pardon. *"Let the people turn from their wicked deeds. Let them banish from their minds the very thought of doing wrong! Let them turn to the Lord that he may have mercy of them. Yes, turn to our God, for he will abundantly pardon."*

Isaiah 55:7

God gives abundant peace. *"I am leaving you with a gift- peace of mind and heart. And the peace I give isn't like the peace the world gives."*

John 14:27

God gives His grace. *"And our Lord poured out his abundant grace on me and gave me the faith and love which are ours in union with Jesus Christ."*

I Timothy 1:14 (Good News Bible)

God gives abundant truth. *"The Lord God, merciful and gracious, long-suffering, and abundant in goodness and truth."*

Exodus 34:6

Oh, that we could claim these promises and live in the fullness of abundance of God's love and mercy.

We are more familiar with being stingy with our forgiveness, miserly with our money, and selfish with our time.

A woman from one of the world's poorer countries was visiting Toronto. Looking out a window, she asked her hostess, *"Who lives in that house?"* pointing to the garage. The hostess replied, *"No one, that is a house for the car."* The guest was amazed that people could afford a car, much less a house to keep it in.

We not only have material abundance, but as a Christian, I am given the opportunity to enjoy God's abundance.

Do You Want To Get Well?

Step Four   Response

1. Make a list of the material things you have in abundance and thank God for them.

2. Make a list of the ways God has blessed you with His abundance of grace, mercy and love.

3. Think of ways you can share God's abundance with your family and those you meet today.

Step Five   Inspiration: ***How Gracious Are Thy Mercies, Lord***

How gracious are thy mercies, Lord, They hallow all my days;
The gifts of tenderness and love, Inspire my heart to praise.
The growing miracle of faith, Assures me I am thine;
Oh, praise thy name that I can share, This fellowship divine!
How lovely are thy mercies, Lord, The earth, the sky, the sea,
For all things good and beautiful, I offer praise to thee.
For clouds by day and stars by night, For blossoms frail and fair,
For all thy glorious handiwork, My heart is moved to prayer.
How tender are they mercies, Lord, Thy grace when days are long.
And in the lonely midnight hour, Thy precious gift of song.
When I approach the gates of death, And life is at an end,

Mary Kathryn Clark

Thy presence will sustain me still, my Savior and my Friend.

Sybil Leonard Armes, 1964
Arranged by Ralph Vaughan Williams, 1906

Step Six   Relaxation

Breathe in abundance, breathe out stinginess

Step Seven   Commitment

Commit the day to Christ and to the leadership of the Holy Spirit

Step Three

Day Nineteen

The Tediousness of Work

"She finds wool and flax and busily spins it. She is like a merchant's ship; she brings her food from afar. She gets up before dawn to prepare breakfast for her household and plan the day's work for her servant girls. She goes out to inspect a field and buys it; with her earnings she plants a vineyard. She is energetic and strong, a hard worker. She watches for bargains; her lights burn late into the night."

Proverbs 31:13-18

A woman's work is never done. It is tedious and boring. It is difficult to get excited about cleaning the house, washing the dishes, doing the laundry, keeping the family clothed, and managing the schedule for the car pool. There is much repetition and leaves little time for creativity and spontaneity.

Is there any viable solution? First, before you get out of bed, thank God for the privilege of another day to live. Ask Him for specific guidance for each task and ask for Him to multiply the hours of the day in order that your tasks can be accomplished. Have a plan for the day. Some of us are more organized than others, but even if it is difficult for you, jot down a list of priorities for the day. All through the day, check in with

God and give Him thanks for His help. Give Him thanks for your husband and your children and that He has placed you in a family.

Paul in **II Thessalonians 3:6-10** says this about work. *"And now dear brothers and sisters, we give you this command with the authority of our Lord Jesus Christ: Stay away from any Christian who lives in idleness and doesn't follow the tradition of hard work we gave you. For you know that you ought to follow our example. We were never lazy when we were with you. We never accepted food from anyone without paying for it. We worked hard day and night so that we would not be a burden to any of you. It wasn't that we didn't have the right to ask you to feed us, but we wanted to give you an example to follow. Even while we were with you, we gave you the rule: 'Whoever does not work should not eat.'"*

Sometimes parents will say that they don't want their children to have to work as hard as they did in their childhood. Work is a sacred privilege, and we should not deny anyone the right to work. With children, we should require that they share in the work in the home in which they live.

Yes, we all get tired or bored with our work. Yes, we fantasize that we would love to go to work if we could have a different job. Yes, we fantasize that we would not mind cleaning the house if we had a bigger and nicer house. Yes, we fantasize that we would not mind working or cleaning after we come back from a three-week cruise.

Do You Want To Get Well?

Step Four   Response

1. Describe your present attitude about work.

2. What is the least favorite thing you have to do?

3. Make a plan for today by setting priorities.

Step Five   Inspiration: ***Trading My Sorrows***

I'm trading my sorrows, I'm trading my shame
I'm laying them down, For the joy of the Lord
I'm trading my sickness, I 'm trading my pain
I' m laying them down, For the joy of the Lord
We say yes Lord, yes Lord, yes, yes Lord
Yes Lord, yes Lord, yes, yes Lord
Yes Lord, yes Lord, yes, yes Lord Amen.
I am pressed, but not crushed, Persecuted not abandoned
Struck down but not destroyed,
I am blessed beyond the curse
For His promise will endure
That His joy is gonna be my strength.
Though the sorrow may last for the night
His joy comes in the morning.

Darrell Evans

Mary Kathryn Clark

Step Six   Relaxation

Breathe in mindfulness, breathe out frustration

Step Seven   Commitment

Commit your day to Christ and to the leadership of the Holy Spirit

Step Three

Day Twenty

The Struggle of Surrender

"Do not be stubborn, as they were (your ancestors and relatives who abandoned the Lord), but submit yourselves to the Lord."

II Chronicles 30:8

"So humble yourselves before God. Resist the Devil, and he will flee from you."

James 4:7

"For the Lord's sake, accept all authority."

I Peter 2:13

We most likely have a negative view of surrender. We are reminded that to surrender in war is to admit defeat and wave the white flag.

In our relationships, we are into wanting to win each battle. We even keep count at times as to how many times we won and how many times we lost. The loser in any relationship is not likely to be happy in the relationship. No individual or no team likes to be thought of as a loser.

Mary Kathryn Clark

Jesus said if we want to be His follower, we must deny self. No, that doesn't mean give up our God-given personality. It means to give up the right to rule and control our own life and give that right to God. Every Christian fights this battle daily because we are selfish, and we want our way and are convinced that our way is the best. The third step of the Twelve Step program of Alcoholic Anonymous is *"Made a decision to turn our will and our lives over to the care of God as we understood him."* It is not accidental that *will* comes before our *lives*. It is much more difficult to turn our wills over than to turn our lives over...

"Overcome not by force, overcome by surrender. The battle is fought, and won, inside ourselves. We must go through it until we learn, until we accept, until we become grateful, until we are set free. For today, trust and gratitude are sufficient," writes Melody Beattie.

Step Four   Response

1. What am I unwilling to let go of?

2. Write about your trust level with God. Do you really believe He wants more good for you than you want for yourself?

3. Which relationship do I have the most difficulty being submissive?

Do You Want To Get Well?

Step Five   Inspiration: *Have Thine Own Way, Lord*

Have Thine Own Way Lord! Have Thine own way!

Thou art the potter, I am the clay; Mold me and make me

After thy will, While I am waiting, Yielded and still.

Have thine own way, Lord! Have thine own way

Search me and try me, Master, today!

Whiter than snow, Lord, Wash me just now,

As in thy presence, Humbly I bow.

Have thine way, Lord! Have thine own way!

Wounded and weary, Help me I pray!

Power, all power, Surely is thine!

Touch me and heal me, Savior divine.

Have thine own way, Lord! Have thine own way!

Hold o'er my being absolute sway!

Fill with thy Spirit, Till all shall see Christ, only always,

Living in me.

Adelaide A Pollard, 1907
George C Stebbins, 1907

Step Six   Relaxation

Breathe in submission, breathe out control

Step Seven   Commitment

Commit your day to Christ and to the leadership of the Holy Spirit

Step Three

Day Twenty-One

The Doom of Fear

"Do not fear anything except the Lord Almighty. He alone is the Holy One. If you fear him you need fear nothing else. He will keep you safe."

Isaiah 8:13-14a

"For God has not given us a spirit of fear and timidity, but of power, love, and self-discipline."

II Timothy 1:7

Have you ever awakened in the night either from a noise or from a dream, and you were afraid? It is a terrible feeling. Your heart is racing and your mind is filled with imagination. Or are you afraid of heights or closed in places?

That fear can become so pronounced that you are labeled with a "phobia".

Fear is powerful and has kept many people from being successful in their jobs and careers. Fear has kept many inventions from being known because the person was afraid of taking a risk. Relationships have ceased because of the fear of failure.

This is a powerful admonition. *"Don't project an old fear on a new day."* Many days have been ruined in our lives because we did just that. We were hanging on to old fears, and they robbed us of new dreams. In reading the Book of Proverbs, the fear of the Lord is mentioned many times. To one who has the fear of the Lord, the blessings and promises are specific-

"Fear the Lord and depart from evil... It will be <u>health to your flesh and strength to your bones</u>."

Proverbs 3:7-8

"The fear of the Lord is the beginning of wisdom, And the knowledge of the Holy One is understanding. For by me <u>your days will be multiplied and years of life will be added to you</u>."

Proverbs 9:10-11

"But in the fear of the Lord continue all day long; For surely there is a hereafter, <u>And your hope will not be cut off</u>."

Proverbs 23:17-18

"My son, if you receive my words, And treasure my commands within you, so that you incline your ear to wisdom, And apply your heart to understanding; Yes, if you cry out for discernment, And lift up your voice for understanding, If you seek her as silver; and search for her as for hidden treasures; THEN you will understand the fear of the Lord."

Proverbs 2:1-5

Do You Want To Get Well?

Step Four   Response

1. List your greatest fears.

2. What are some of my past fears that affect me today?

3. How do I feel about "fearing the Lord?"

Step Five   Inspiration: ***Have Faith in God***

Have faith in God when your pathway is lonely,
He sees and knows all the way you have trod,
Never alone are the least of His children;
Have faith in God, Have faith in God
Have faith in God when your pray'rs are unanswered,
Your earnest plea, He will never forget,
Wait on the Lord, trust His Word and be patient,
Have faith in God, He'll answer yet.
Have faith in God in your pain and your sorrow,
His heart is touched with your grief and despair;
Cast all your cares and your burdens upon Him,
And leave them there, oh leave them there.
Have faith in God tho all else fail about you;
Have faith in God, He provides for His own,
He cannot fail tho all kingdoms shall perish,
He rules, He reigns upon His throne.

Mary Kathryn Clark

Have faith in God, He's on His throne

Have faith in God, He watches o'er His own;

He cannot fail, He must prevail,

Have faith in God, Have faith in God.

B.B. McKinney, 1934

Step Six   Relaxation

Breathe in unafraid, breathe out afraid

Step Seven   Commitment

Commit your day to Christ and to the leadership of the Holy Spirit

Step Three

Day Twenty-Two

The Efficacy of Prayer

"O God, listen to my cry! Hear my prayer! From the ends of the earth, I will cry to you for help, for my heart is overwhelmed."

Psalm 61:1-2

"O Lord, hear my plea for justice. Listen to my cry for help. Pay attention to my prayer for it comes from an honest heart."

Psalm 17:1

"The Lord is far from the wicked, but he hears the prayers of the righteous."

Proverbs 15:29

Jesus says, *"And now about prayer. When you pray, don't be like the hypocrites who love to pray publicly on street corners and in the synagogues where everyone can see them. I assure you, that is all the reward they will ever get. But when you pray, go away by yourself, shut the door behind you and pray to your Father secretly. Then your Father who knows all secrets, will reward you. When you pray, don't babble on and on as people of other religions do. They think their prayers are answered only by repeating their words again and again. Don't be like them, because your Father knows exactly what you need even before you ask him."*

Matthew 6:5-8

Do we need any more instruction than that for our prayers? Jesus clearly says we need to be alone, and we need to pour out our heart to him. We don't have to beg him or keep asking because he already knows our need.

Prayer is more about my attitude about life, people and relationships than it is about the form or the words or the frequency or the specified time. Prayer is the link between myself and God and that takes different forms daily. Prayer is fluid rather than static. Prayer is growth, not perfection. Prayer is love in action. Prayer is wanting to do what God wants me to do. Prayer is unconditionally loving another. Prayer is giving a word of affirmation instead of criticism. Prayer is having a childlike faith rather than pages of rational reasons. Prayer is always wanting the best for the other person. Prayer will not allow me to keep long accounts. Prayer is forgiveness. Prayer is touching or giving a hug to reassure. Prayer allows God to love and live through me to touch other lives. Prayer is humility. Prayer is authentic living.

Does this help you realize that prayer is not about form or words or frequency?

Prayer is about my daily life. It is about my behavior and my attitude.

Do You Want To Get Well?

Step Four   Response

1. Write a prayer to God describing your feelings and beliefs about prayer.

2. Write an explanation to a child as to what it means to live out your prayers.

3. Write about your deepest need in prayer right now.

Step Five   Inspiration: ***Sweet Hour of Prayer***

Sweet hour of prayer, sweet hour of prayer,
That calls me from a world of care
And bids me at my Father's throne
Make all my wants and wishes known.
In seasons of distress and grief,
My soul has often found relief,
And oft escaped the tempter's snare
By thy return, sweet hour of prayer.
Sweet hour of prayer, sweet hour of prayer,
Thy wings shall my petition bear
To him whose truth and faithfulness
Engage the waiting soul to bless.
And since he bids me seek his face,
Believe his word and trust his grace,

Mary Kathryn Clark

I'll cast on him my every care,

And wait for thee, sweet hour of prayer.

Sweet hour of prayer, sweet of prayer,

May I thy consolation share,

Till from Mount Pisgah's lofty height,

I view my home and take my flight.

This robe of flesh I'll drop and rise

To seize the everlasting prize;

And shout while passing thro' the air,

Farewell, farewell, sweet hour of prayer.

William Walford, 1840
William B. Bradbury, 1861

Step Six   Relaxation

Breathe in behavior, breathe out words

Step Seven   Commitment

Commit your day to Christ and to the leadership of the Holy Spirit

Step Three

Day Twenty-Three

The Difficulty with Communication

We currently live in the most advanced stages of technology this world has ever known. We are addicted to e-mail, cell phones, iPads, and the need to "be in touch". We can be tracked by cell phone as to our presence, and we can use a GPS which will tell us every turn we need to make to reach our destination.

But, in spite of all of this, probably the greatest need we have is to be heard. We are so tuned into technology that we don't hear people when they speak to us. We don't have time to listen even to those who are the most significant people in our lives. Teenagers are starved to have someone listen to them; preschoolers need someone who will listen as they describe their "work of art"; wives need their husbands to hear how stressful their day has been; husbands need their wives to listen to their gigantic problems and concerns.

"Everyone has a cry within for justice for being." We hear this cry by listening.

Listening is an investment in another. Listening is loving another into being. Listening is a gift we give to others.

"Listening requires silence, patience,

the tuning out of other sounds, focusing on one person,

getting information, hearing the word that person is saying.

When we listen, we create an environment for each other of

understanding, consideration, and cooperation.

I serve the other through my willingness

to let that other, have personal rights in likes,

tasks, tastes, habits, opinions.

Listening helps me accept the other

without attempting to change that other into my own image."

As you read these lines, can you see how difficult it is to listen and to communicate?

I believe effective communication is a skill which has to be practiced. One of the first things to learn is that when you attempt to express your needs or feelings, always begin the sentence with "I". No one can argue with how you feel. When you begin a sentence with "you", you will usually incite an angry reaction because the other person hears that you are blaming him for the problem.

Communication takes time. Couples have to plan a priority time on their calendar to have a date night so they can communicate. Families have to plan a family night on their day timer so that the children can have an opportunity to talk to their parents.

In today's fast pace, that is the only chance people will have to communicate. In our history, families used the dinner hour to talk with each other. Research tells us that many families never sit down to a

Do You Want To Get Well?

meal together at home, maybe in a fast-food restaurant which is not conducive to intimate conversation.

Step Four   Response

1. Who do I wish would listen to me? Who do I need to listen to?

2. What do I need to do to become a better listener?

3. Did I listen to God yesterday? Am I going to take time to listen to Him today? If my answer is No, then why?

Step Five   Inspiration: ***What a Friend We Have in Jesus***

> *What a friend we have in Jesus, All our sins and griefs to bear!*
> *What a privilege to carry, Everything to God in prayer!*
> *Oh, what peace we often forfeit, O what needless pain we bear,*
> *All because we do not carry, Everything to God in prayer.*
> *Have we trials and temptations? Is there trouble anywhere?*
> *We should never be discouraged, Take it to the Lord in prayer.*
> *Can we find a friend so faithful, Who will all our sorrows share?*
> *Jesus knows our every weakness, Take it to the Lord in prayer.*
> *Are we weak and heavy laden, cumbered with a load of care?*

Mary Kathryn Clark

Precious Savior, still our refuge; Take it to the Lord in prayer.

Do thy friends despise, forsake thee?

Take it to the Lord in prayer.

In his arms he'll take and shield thee;

Thou wilt find a solace there.

Joseph Scriven, 1855
Charles C. Converse, 1868

Step Six   Relaxation

Breathe in listen, breathe out not interested

Step Seven   Commitment

Commit your day to Christ and to the leadership of the Holy Spirit

Step Three

Day Twenty-Four

The Destruction of Anger

"And don't sin by letting anger gain control over you. Don't let the sun go down while you are still angry, for anger gives a mighty foothold to the Devil."

Ephesians 4:26-27

"Don't be quick-tempered, for anger is the friend of fools."

Ecclesiastes 7:9

"Keep away from angry, short-tempered people, or you will learn to be like them and endanger your soul."

Proverbs 22:24-25

Anger is a God-given emotion. Anger is a natural response when we have been hurt, abused, or rejected. Anger is a secondary emotion and underneath are the primary emotions of hurt and fear. When I experience anger, first I need to identify the hurt or the fear. I need to acknowledge my authentic feelings and seek God's help in dealing with them. The answer may be to confront, write a letter and burn it, slam a door, yell, beat a pillow or work out in a fitness room. There is nothing wrong with

Mary Kathryn Clark

expressing your anger as long as you don't hurt yourself or anyone else. Being grateful, being positive, being healthy, does not mean that we never feel angry.

I fear that the church has taught that getting angry is wrong for a Christian. Thus, feelings are stuffed and begin to wreak havoc with our souls. I believe that every emotion is carried in our veins and arteries which have a cumulative memory. We need to deal with our strong feelings before the sun sets, or else they will begin to affect our spiritual and physical health.

Anger is a potent, frightening emotion. It can force us to make important decisions. It can be an identifier that we need to address a problem with another person. Our anger does not go away. If we don't face our angry feelings today, we will need to face them tomorrow. They sit in layers under the surface; waiting for us to become strong enough to deal with them. We may be afraid of our anger and that if we let it surface, we would be out of control.

Melody Beattie writes this prayer to deal with our anger.

"God, help my hidden or repressed angry feelings to surface. Help me have the courage to face them. Help me understand how I need to take care of myself with the people I feel anger toward. Help me stop telling myself something is wrong with me when people victimize me and I feel angry about the victimization. I can trust my anger to signal problems that need my attention."

"Understand this, my brethren, let everyone be quick to listen, slow to talk, slow to get angry; for man's anger does not promote God's righteousness"

James 1:19-20 (Modern Language)

Step Four   Response

1. When was the last time you were really angry?

2. How did you handle the anger?

3. Ask God to reveal to you if you are clinging to some old wounds which hurt?

Step Five   Inspiration: ***Change my Heart O God***

Change my heart, O God, Make it ever true,
Change my heart, O God, May I be like you
You are the Potter, I am the clay;
Mold me and make me, This is what I pray.
Change my heart, O God, Make it ever true,
Change my heart, O God, May I be like you.
You are the Potter, I am the clay;
Mold me and make me, This is what I pray.

Mary Kathryn Clark

> *Change my heart, O God, Make it ever true,*
> *Change my heart, O God, May I be like you.*

Eddie Espinosa

Step Six   Relaxation

Breathe in acceptance, breathe out anger

Step Seven   Commitment

Commit your day to Christ and to the leadership of the Holy Spirit

Step Three

Day Twenty-Five

The Seriousness of Example

"For I have given you an example, that ye should do as I have done to you."

John 13:15

"And you became imitators of us and of the Lord, for you received the word in much affliction, with joy inspired by the Holy Spirit..."

I Thessalonians 1:6

Albert Schweitzer wrote, *"Example is not the main thing in influencing others. It is the only thing."*

This is an awesome challenge for parents to know that it is not what they buy their children or what schools they attend, but it is the example of the parents which exerts the greatest influence. It is what the children observe in non-verbal communication that sometimes yells out over the words they speak. A child is blessed if he can look to his parents for his Christian model and example.

A child is blessed if he has Christian grandparents who love him and provide a good model for him.

Mary Kathryn Clark

To be a worthy example, I must think before I speak. I must keep my cup filled so that I don't react from an empty cup. I must weigh my words and say less. Sometimes silence is the most important message I can send.

It can bring tears to my eyes, to watch a small child try to walk in his father's footsteps on the beach. To observe a little girl try to dress like her mother. To see a child try to model a Christian teacher.

Be careful what you do and say. You may be the only Bible some will read. You never know who is watching and who will be influenced by your example.

Do but set the example yourself, and I will follow you. *"Example is the best precept."*

Step Four   Response

1. Write about people who have been positive examples in your life.

2. Describe characteristics in your life that you feel are good examples for others.

3. Describe characteristics in your life that are not good examples for others.

Do You Want To Get Well?

Step Five   Inspiration: **Sanctuary**

Lord, prepare me to be a Sanctuary,

Pure and holy, tried and true

With thanksgiving, I'll be a living Sanctuary for you.

It is you, Lord, who came to save

The heart and soul of every man

It is you, Lord, who knows my weakness

Who gives me strength,

With thine own hand Lord, prepare me to be a Sanctuary,

Pure and holy, tried and true

With thanksgiving, I'll be a living Sanctuary for you.

Lead me, Lord, from temptation,

Purify me from within

Fill my heart with your holy spirit, Take away my sin.

Lord, prepare me to be a Sanctuary,

Pure and holy, tried and true

With thanksgiving, I'll be a living Sanctuary for you.

John W. Thompson
Randy Scruggs

Step Six   Relaxation

Breathe in good example, breathe out bad example

Step Seven   Commitment

Commit your day to Christ and to the leadership of the Holy Spirit

Step Three

Day Twenty-Six

The Tenacity of Patience

"In your patience, possess ye your souls."

Luke 21:19

"We can rejoice, too, when we run into problems and trials for, we know that they are good for us- they help us learn to be patient... And patience develops strength of character in us and helps us trust God more each time we use it until finally our hope and faith are strong and steady. Then when that happens, we are able to hold our heads high no matter what happens and know that all is well, for we know how dearly God loves us and we feel this warm love everywhere within us because God has given us the Holy Spirit to fill our hearts with his love."

Romans 5:3-5 (Living Bible)

"Wherefore seeing we also are compassed about with so great a cloud of witnesses, let us lay aside every weight, and the sin which doth so easily beset us, and let us run with patience the race that is set before us."

Hebrews 12:1

Mary Kathryn Clark

When we pray to God for something, we usually want the answer yesterday! Patience is not our strong asset. We are living in a fast paced society where there is road rage if we have to wait a few seconds in traffic and even the microwave seems slow. Our children know nothing of having to wait for a toy until there is money. Young married couples want to start out in the same kind of home their parents live in now. People want to start at the top of the career ladder and not work their way up.

"Wisely and slow: they stumble that run fast," says William Shakespeare.

Perhaps Shakespeare would observe today that we have many people who are running fast and stumbling. Patience is a virtue that seems to be a thing of the past.

We fear if we are patient, we will lose the race.

Notice that all the figures who appear in the first pages of Luke's Gospel are waiting. Zechariah and Elizabeth are waiting. Mary is waiting. Simeon and Anna, who were there at the temple when Jesus was brought in, were waiting. And at the beginning, all those people in some way or other heard the words, *"Do not be afraid. I have something good to say to you."*

A Jewish writer, Simone Weil, said, *"Waiting patiently in expectation is the foundation of the spiritual life."* If we want to get well, we have to learn patience.

Do You Want To Get Well?

Step Four   Response

1. In what areas am I the most impatient?

2. Can you think of a time when you prayed diligently for something and it did not happen and you realized that by waiting for God, the result was much better?

3. Try today to pace your activities. Do everything you do a little bit slower. Eat more slowly. Drive more slowly. Get groceries more slowly... Take a little time to talk to your children. Spend a few more minutes with your husband. Make mental notes during the day what it is like to not rush with everything you do.

Step Five   Inspiration: ***Take Time to Be Holy***

Take time to be holy, speak oft with thy Lord
Abide in Him always, and feed on His word.
Make friends of God's children, help those who are weak,
Forgetting in nothing His blessing to seek.
Take time to be holy, the world rushes on,
Spend much time in secret, with Jesus alone,
By looking to Jesus, like Him thou shalt be;
Thy friends in thy conduct His likeness shall see.
Take time to be holy, let Him be thy Guide;

Mary Kathryn Clark

And run not before Him, whatever betide,

In joy or in sorrow, still follow the Lord,

And, looking to Jesus, still trust in His Word.

Take time to be holy, be calm in thy soul,

Each thought and each motive beneath His control.

Thus led by His spirit to fountains of love,

That soon shall be fitted for service above.

William D. Longstaff ca... 1882

Step Six   Relaxation

Breathe in patience, breathe out hurry

Step Seven   Commitment

Commit your day to Christ and to the leadership of the Holy Spirit

Step Three

Day Twenty-Seven

The Toll of Guilt and Resentment

"If someone has done you wrong, do not repay with a wrong.... Never take revenge, my friends, but instead let God's anger do it. For the Scripture says, 'I will take revenge, I will pay back, says the Lord.'"

Romans 12:17-19

"Nothing on earth can consume a man more completely than the passion of resentment."

Friedrich Nietzsche

Holding on to a resentment is like taking a drink of poison yourself and hoping it will kill the person you resent. Resentment can eat away at our spiritual power and destroy it.

Guilt has the same power to destroy. When we hold on to our guilt, we negate the fact that Jesus died on the Cross to take away our sins and guilt. We make his death useless if we tenaciously hold on to our guilt.

Lewis Carroll writes, *"The horror of the moment"* the King said, (in angry resentment)*"I shall never, never forget."*

Mary Kathryn Clark

"You will, though," said the Queen, *"If you don't make a memorandum of it."*

Oh, if we could throw away, destroy, burn, shred all of our memorandums. If we could take all of the "if only's" and the "I should haves" and toss them completely out of our lives. We would be able to drop the burden of guilt and resentment we have carried for years. We would know a new freedom in Christ.

Perhaps the most difficult person we have to forgive is ourselves.

"I have come that they might have life, and that they might have it more abundantly."

John 10:10

Step Four   Response

1. What resentment is eating away at your heart?

2. What guilt is robbing you of peace and serenity?

3. Am I experiencing the abundant life? What is keeping me from that experience?

Do You Want To Get Well?

Step Five   Inspiration: ***Glorify Thy Name***

Father, we love You, We worship and adore You
Glorify Thy name, Glorify Thy name.
Glorify Thy name in all the earth.
Jesus, we love You, We worship and adore You
Glorify Thy name, Glorify Thy name.
Glorify Thy name in all the earth.
Spirit, we love You, We worship and adore You
Glorify Thy name in all the earth.
Glorify Thy name, Glorify Thy name.

Donna Adkins

Step Six   Relaxation

Breathe in release, breathe out toll

Step Seven   Commitment

Commit your day to Christ and to the leadership of the Holy Spirit

Step Three

Day Twenty-Eight

The Centrality of Purpose

"For I know the plans for you, says the Lord. They are plans for good and not for evil, to give you a future and a hope."

Jeremiah 29:11

If you are going to get well, one of the first things you have to change in your life is your attitude about why you are here. You have to come to the point of belief that God created you for a purpose, and once you have found that purpose, everything you do and say has importance to God and His plan. There are no longer any accidents in your life.

Everything that happens has an expressed purpose and meaning. There is no longer a division between sacred and secular. Everything is sacred.

Jesus struggled with this before His death. He prayed fervently in the Garden, *"My Father, if it be possible, let this cup pass from me, nevertheless, not as I will, but as thou wilt."* **Mathew 26:39** (Revised Standard) He was willing to serve the purpose for which He was created. Before God created Adam and Eve, He knew the whole purpose and plan and He knew at that time that Jesus, His only Son, was going to have to sacrifice His life for the sin of all mankind.

Mary Kathryn Clark

Leslie Weatherhead in the little book, <u>The Will of God</u>, says there are three wills. First, the perfect will, second, the permissive will and third, the ultimate will. If Adam and Eve had not sinned, we would have stayed in God's perfect will. But since the fall of man, God has used His permissive will for man. For the committed Christian, there is absolutely NOTHING that comes into his life that is not known by God and that He will not use for good. Nothing can come through to hurt, harm, or touch a committed Christian until or unless it is filtered through God's permissive will.

A committed Christian must be convinced that his time here on earth is ordained. *"For after David had served his generation according to the will of God, he died and was buried and his body decayed."*

Acts 13:36 (Living Bible)

Beth Moore in her powerful testimony says that her time on earth is ordained because she lives in the first generation where child abuse can be openly discussed. She believes that her story is ripe for the times because she can share and help so many other women who have suffered abuse.

Joseph said to his brothers, *"Don't be afraid of me. Am I God, to judge and punish you? As far as I am concerned, God turned into good what you meant for evil, for He brought me to this high position I have today so that I could save the lives of many people. No, don't be afraid. Indeed, I myself will take care of you and your families."*

Genesis 50:19-21

Do You Want To Get Well?

No matter who sought to do you harm, who sought to bring you pain, God can heal you and the horrendous situations can be used for good. This is true in my life. I was beaten by my father when I was eighteen; was the caretaker for my husband of thirty-two years who had Alzheimer's for the last five years of his life; was in an abusive marriage with a recovering alcoholic and drug abuser for sixteen months; experienced deprivation from parents who could not give me the nurturing needed and who had no idea how to foster independence in a child. Every one of these life happenings has served me well in my role as a professional counselor. When I say I have experienced that, there is immediate bonding with the client. God brought good out of the pain in order that I could share my story of healing and purpose. I never cease to be amazed at the numerous times God has brought people into my world who needed to hear my story. God is good all the time—All the time God is good.

Step Four   Response

1. List some of the painful experiences in your life.

2. On a continuum of 1 to 10, where are you in dealing with those experiences? 1 means you are bitter and resentful that these things happened to you... and 10 means you have experienced God's healing in that area.

Mary Kathryn Clark

3. If your answers were in the low range, plan a way to deal with the pain. If your answers were in the high range, write a prayer of gratitude for the way God is using your life today.

Step Five   Inspiration: ***Shout to the North***

> *Men of faith, rise up and sing, Of the great and glorious King*
> *You are strong when you feel weak, in your brokenness complete*
> *Shout to the north and the south, Sing to the east and the west*
> *Jesus is Savior to all, Lord of Heaven and Earth*
> *Rise up, women of the truth, Stand and sing to broken hearts*
> *Who can know the healing power, Of our awesome King of Love*
> *We've been through fire, We've been through rain*
> *We've been refined by the power of His name*
> *We've fallen deeper in love with You*
> *You've burned the truth on our lips*
> *Rise up, church, with broken wings*
> *Fill this place with songs again*
> *Of our God who reigns on high, By His grace again we'll fly*

Martin Smith

Step Six   Relaxation

Breathe in purpose, breathe out existing

Do You Want To Get Well?

Step Seven   Commitment

Commit your day to Christ and to the leadership of the Holy Spirit

Step Three

Day Twenty-Nine

The Craving for Relationships

The most important of all relationships is the recognition that I am a child of God.

"How great is the love the Father has lavished on us, that we should be called the children of God."

I John 3:1

"If I have internalized this relationship with my heavenly Father, I have a solid basis for all other relationships because all my hurt and rejection are filtered through the love of God. In human relationships, there is the likelihood that I am going to hurt and be hurt; that I am going to reject and be rejected; that I am going to give pain and receive pain." That is the nature of human relationships, and we need God's love as a buffer to protect us.

Anne Morrow Lindbergh makes these comments on human love. *"When you love someone, you do not love them all the time, in exactly the same way, from moment to moment. It is an impossibility. It is even a lie to pretend to. And yet this is exactly what most of us demand. We have so little faith in the flow of the tide and resist in terror the ebb. We are afraid it will never return. We insist on permanency, on duration, on*

Mary Kathryn Clark

continuity; when the only continuity possible in life as in love, is in growth, in fluidity, in freedom, in the sense that the dancers are free, barely touching as they pass, but partners in the same pattern."

I am grateful for the wonderful relationships in my life. Each has challenged me to grow toward becoming a whole person. I believe each significant person gives us a gift, and I am the person I am today because of the many gifts I have been given.

Relationships enable us to know who we are.

Relationships challenge us to be the best person we can be for the other person.

Relationships have the capacity to bring out our "dark side".

Relationships teach us patience, tolerance, flexibility, wisdom, perseverance and humility.

In <u>Listening to Your Life</u>, Frederick Buechner vividly describes relationships in today's society. *"Our society is filled with people for whom the sexual relationship is one where body meets body but where person fails to meet person; where the immediate need for sexual gratification is satisfied but where the deeper need for companionship and understanding is left untouched. The result is that the relationship leads not to fulfillment but to a half-conscious sense of incompleteness, of inner loneliness, which is so much the sickness of our time. The desire to know another's nakedness is really the desire to know the other fully as a person. It is the desire to know and to be known not just sexually but as a total human being. It is the desire for a relationship where each one gives not just of his body but of his self, body and spirit both, for the other's gladness."*

"Love is a friendship that has caught fire. It is quiet understanding, mutual confidence, sharing and forgiving. It is loyalty through the good times and bad. It settles for less than perfection and makes allowances for weaknesses."

"Love is content with the present, it hopes for the future, and doesn't brood over the past. It's the day-in, day-out chronicles of irritations, problems, compromises, small disappointments, big victories and common goals."

"If you have love in your life, it can make up for a great many things you lack... If you don't have it, no matter what else there is, it is not enough."

Step Four   Response

1. List ten significant people in your life and beside each name, list the gift they gave you.

2. List five people and the gifts you have given them.

3. Write about the person with whom you have the most difficult relationship.

Mary Kathryn Clark

Step Five   Inspiration: ***You'll Never Walk Alone***

When you walk through a storm, Hold your head up high
And don't be afraid of the dark.
At the end of the storm is a golden sky
And the sweet silver song of a lark
Walk on through the wind, Walk on through the rain
Though your dreams be tossed and blown
Walk on, walk on with hope in your heart and
you'll never walk alone
You'll never walk alone
Walk on, walk on with hope in your heart and
you'll never walk alone
You'll never walk alone.

Rodgers and Hammerstein, 1945

Step Six   Relaxation

Breathe in healing, breathe out hurt

Step Seven   Commitment

Commit your day to Christ and to the leadership of the Holy Spirit

Step Three

Day Thirty

The Foolishness of Expectations

Have you ever said - *"They knew what I wanted. Why didn't they do it? I even told them what I wanted and needed, and they still didn't do it."*

Expectations are premeditated resentments.

If I did not have expectations, I would not have fertile ground for resentment.

We expect others to behave in certain ways. They do not, and we are disappointed.

All of us have needs, and no one human person can meet those needs. *"Turning to an alcoholic (or a dysfunctional person) for affection and support can be like going to the hardware store for bread."* If you turn only to your husband or wife to meet all of your needs, because of their own deprivation, they may not be able to meet your needs. A woman needs to have one or two close women friends with whom she can share. Women have a great capacity to nurture, love, care and listen to all of the details which are important to women. A man needs to have quality time with men on a regular basis to discuss their issues, needs and to develop their spiritual qualities.

To be a virtuous woman, one needs to eliminate those expectations that demand another to change. We have to be willing to let go of those fantasies of how you want another to behave. We have to give up the arrogance that we know what is best for another. We have to be realistic about who can meet our needs.

The fewer resentments we have, the more contentment we will have and the more charity for others.

"Let all bitterness and wrath, and anger, and clamor and evil speaking be put away from you, with all malice. And be ye kind one to another, tenderhearted, forgiving one another, even as God for Christ's sake hath forgiven you."

Ephesians 4:31-32

Step Four Response

1. Who has disappointed you because they did not meet your needs?

2. Whose behavior have you tried to change?

3. Pray specifically for those people, and ask God to give you His perspective of those people.

Do You Want To Get Well?

Step Five   Inspiration: *You Raise Me Up*

When I am down and oh my soul so weary
When troubles come and my heart burdened be
Then I am still and wait here in the silence
Until you come and sit awhile with me.
You raise me up, so I can stand on mountains
You raise me up to walk on stormy seas
You raise me up, so I can stand on mountains
You raise me up to walk on stormy seas
I am strong when I am on your shoulders
You raise me up to more than I can be.
You raise me up to more than I can be.

Josh Groban

Step Six   Relaxation

Breathe in reality, breathe out unreality

Step Seven   Commitment

Commit your day to Christ and to the leadership of the Holy Spirit

Step Three

Day Thirty-One

The Cost of Love

"Beloved, let us love one another for love is of God; and everyone that loveth is born of God and knoweth God. He that loveth not knoweth not God; for God is love."

I John 4:7-8

"For God so loved the world that he gave his only begotten Son that whosoever believeth in him should not perish but have everlasting life."

John 3:16

God paid the ultimate sacrifice of unconditional love when He gave His only son to die for our transgressions. No price could have been higher.

It is easy to love the lovable; it is a challenge to love the unlovable. Jesus says we have no reward if we love only the lovable. Any sinner can do that. Jesus calls us to a deeper and more sacrificial love.

Frederick Buechner describes love in this way, *"To lose yourself in another's arms, or in another's company; or in suffering for all men who suffer; including the ones who inflict suffering upon you to lose yourself in such ways is to find yourself. Is what it's all about... Is what love is."*

Mary Kathryn Clark

Often our love is motivated by what is in it for me. Our love can be selfish and manipulative. Our love can be motivated by all the wrong reasons.

Brennan Manning writes of the unconditional love of Jesus. He says, *"God cannot stop loving you because God is love. There is ABSOLUTELY nothing we can do, say, or think that Jesus does not understand. Jesus invites us to come to Him when we are wounded, angry, and lonely. He says I love you as you are, NOT as you should be, because you will never be as you should be. When we surrender to Christ, He says, 'I thought you would have made more mistakes than you did.'"*

When I heard Brennan Manning paraphrase what Jesus might say to me when I surrender to Him, I cried. What incredible love! What compassion!

And if I accept God's unconditional love for me, then I am challenged to go and love as He has loved me. We can forgive all those people in our lives who are less than perfect.

That is what Jesus does for us.

"Regardless of what else you put on, wear love: It's your basic, all-purpose garment. Never be without it."

Colossians 3:14 (MSG)

Do You Want To Get Well?

Step Four   Response

1. Who are the people in my life who have unconditionally loved me?

2. Who is in desperate need of my loving them?

3. Write your definition of unconditional love.

Step Five   Inspiration: *O Love of God*

The love of God is greater far than tongue or pen can ever tell;
It goes beyond the highest star; And reaches to the lowest hell;
The guilty pair; bowed down with care. God gave His Son to win;
His erring child He reconciled, And pardoned from his sin.
When hoary times shall pass away, and heavenly thrones and kingdoms
fall,
When man who here refuse to pray, On rocks and hills and mountains
call,
God's love so sure, shall still endure,
All measureless and strong; Redeeming grace to Adam's races--
The Saints' and angel's song.
Could we with ink the ocean fill,
And were the skies of parchment made,
Were every stalk on earth a quill. And every man a scribe by trade;
To write the love of God above, Would drain the ocean dry;
Nor could the scroll contain the whole,

143

Mary Kathryn Clark

Though stretched from sky to sky.
O love of God, how rich and pure! How measureless and strong.
It shall forevermore endure-- The saints' and angels' and song.

Frederick Martin Lehman

Step Six   Relaxation

Breathe in unconditional love, breathe out conditional love

Step Seven   Commitment

Commit your day to Christ and to the leadership of the Holy Spirit

Checklist for New Year

1. I don't waste time feeling sorry for myself - feeling that life is not fair.
2. I don't give away my power - others can't take away my confidence.
3. I don't shy away from change.
4. I don't waste energy on things I can't control.
5. I don't worry about pleasing others- only about pleasing God.
6. I don't fear taking calculated risks.
7. I don't dwell on the past.
8. I don't make the same mistakes over and over.
9. I don't resent other people's success.
10. I don't give up after failure.
11. I don't fear alone time.
12. I don't feel that the world owes me something.
13. I don't expect immediate results.
14. I don't want the New Year to be like the last year. I want to grow more like Christ.

The Cathedral of Leaves

A gentle breeze moves among the limbs and leaves,

The birds sing to each other and to all who listen,

The azure blue of the sky can be seen through the tree tops,

And the warmth of the morning sun is pleasing to the body.

The tall stately trees have formed this cathedral for years.

They've never known the noise, pollution and crowdedness of the city.

They tower in strength and yet the gentle breeze can make them bend to
and fro.

Help me to be consumed by this cathedral of leaves;

Help me to bend gently with the pressures of responsibility;

Help me to sing softly to myself and to others who live near me;

Help me to lend richness of the blues and greens and browns to the world
I trod daily;

Help me to be as still and quiet as these mountainsides.

I thank you, God, for this cathedral of leaves.

For You made this place for rest and solace for your children,

You intended all of earth to be as beautiful as this cathedral.

Only man, without You, has destroyed the sacred places.

May this one and all others like it be preserved for all the ages

Because man was created to live in the Cathedral of the leaves.

MKC

We Are Wonderfully Made

"I praise you because I am fearfully and wonderfully made."

Psalm 139:14 NIV

We can only imagine the concentrated thoughts that occupied the divine Mind and the gentle, skilled touch of the divine Hand that first shaped man from the dust. Where did the Creator begin? Did He start with a skeletal frame? Did He then cover it with an outside layer of skin, which at no place is thicker than three-sixteenths of an inch, is packed with nerve endings to enable man to feel the outside world, and is virtually waterproof? Into the skin stretched over the frame did He next place the heart that pumps seventy-two times a minute, forty million times a year? When did He hang the lungs in their sealed compartments so that the rivers of blood necessary for life can deposit the carbon dioxide and pick up oxygen to be carried to every single one of the more than twenty-six trillion cells in the body? When did He place the brain inside the bony skull and program it to send messages that travel faster than three hundred miles an hour along the nervous system to the entire body? Truly, we are fearfully and wonderfully and lovingly and personally created by an awe-inspiring, loving Creator!

Anne Graham Lotz

Willing to Be Whole

"Do you want to get well?"

John 5:6 NIV

Jesus didn't ask the man beside the pool of Bethesda, *"Do you need to get well?"* But, *"Do you want to get well?"* There was no preliminary introduction or social niceties or even social conversation, just a Stranger asking a question that would have had a very obvious answer. Surely without question, anyone who was a paralytic would want to be able to walk.

But Jesus knew that it's easy for physical weakness and mental depression and a lifetime of hopelessness to rob a man of his willingness to do anything about it. It would be less demanding in many ways for the man to be carried about by others. His paralysis absolved him from taking responsibility in life.

Jesus knows one of the greatest barriers to our faith is often our unwillingness to be made whole-our unwillingness to live without excuse for our spiritual smallness and immaturity. And so the question He asked was very relevant then and still is today, *"Do you want to get well?"*

Anne Graham Lotz

About the Author

Mary Kathryn Clark is an educator and licensed professional counselor. Her thirty-year teaching experience included teaching English and History in public high schools and directing a private church kindergarten. She organized a private preschool program for special needs children before Virginia public schools had special education programs. For eighteen years she served as supervisor of reading and curriculum planning for a city school system. She taught courses at several universities and was an instructor of elementary education at Shenandoah University.

In 1986 she met the requirements for licensure as a professional counselor in the State of Virginia, and had a successful private practice in three communities. Though her primary work was with women's issues, she also counseled with men, couples, children and families.

As a minister's wife for thirty-two years, she planned retreats and religious activities for children, youth and adults. She taught an adult Sunday School class of women for twenty-five years. Life has afforded many experiences of growth which include being an only child, having step children and no natural children, being a caretaker for her husband who was a victim of Alzheimer's for five years, looking for love in an abusive relationship, and finally experiencing the "dark night of the soul." All of these growth experiences propelled her into deep soul-searching and the realization that God can heal all wounds.

She has had articles published in "Opening Doors", a magazine for parents and teachers, Board of Christian Education, The United Presbyterian Church, Philadelphia, Pennsylvania, and "The Forum", Al-Anon Family Group Headquarters, New York.

She has published three previous books, Colors of His Grace, Colors of His Abundance and In the Morning...Joy.

Her bachelor's degree was from the University of Richmond in Richmond Virginia and her Master's Degree and the Advanced Graduate Degree was from the University of Virginia, Charlottesville, Virginia. The post graduate work in counseling was completed at James Madison University, Harrisonburg, Virginia.

Mary Kathryn currently lives in Winchester, Virginia.

Her personal email is mkclark1@comcast.net.

Printed in the USA
CPSIA information can be obtained
at www.ICGtesting.com
LVHW051223261023
762202LV00016B/987